Graveyard
Blues

PHILLIP DANNA

PAGE PUBLISHING, INC.
New York, NY

First originally published by Page Publishing, Inc. 2016

ISBN 978-1-68289-325-8 (pbk)
ISBN 978-1-68289-326-5 (digital)

Printed in the United States of America

Contents

Chapter 2

Chapter 3

Chapter 4

Chapter 5

Chapter 6

Dark Finger of Night

by Lloyd and Margaret Winstead

As fingers night chase the light from the sky,
Children tucked in beds come running during graveyard shift.
Meanwhile the graveyard phones have started to ring.
The phones continue to ring.
What is this night going to bring?
During graveyard shift
Officers witness every imaginable society's crazies come alive.
Types of prostitutes, drug dealers, homeless, cesspools,
the ghettos where gang bangers try to rule the streets.
His bedroom door opens slowly with the creak in terror.
These are crimes the officer sees every night.
They try hardest to keep the public fatigue.
The hours pass subconsciously, and they must hon-
estly ask which call will be the last.

Acknowledgments

To Lloyd and Margaret Winstead for contributing the poem.

To Vivian Beatty for her assistance with typing and editing the book.

To Brian and Mary English for assistance with the introduction.

To the many people that I worked with during the thirty years of service in the San Bernardino County Sheriff Department

Dedication

This book is dedicated to all the peace officers who are working the midnight shift when danger is at its peak. The graveyard shift, as it is referred to by most people that work this shift, encompasses times from 2400 hours to 0700 hours (12:00 a.m. to 7:00 a.m.).

Visit the police memorial and take your entire family to look at the many names of the brave men and women who patrol your streets and neighborhood during the graveyard shift and all shifts.

Introduction

Law enforcement officers all over the world start their shift in basically the same fashion. They park their personal cars behind a safe, secure gate and enter the building and go to the locker room to change from their civilian clothes into their uniforms. All those assigned to the shift engage in small talk and report to each other those important events that had the most effect on their day. After dressing into their sharply pressed uniforms and donning the tools of their trade—a large belt referred to as a Sam Brown, which contains a firearm holster containing a weapon, handcuffs in a case, a handcuff key, whistle, and baton or night stick as it is commonly referred to. The wise officer, at the time, would also have a leather case attached to the belt with a mini tape recorder inside, flashlight, and report clipboard in hand as the shift personnel move toward the briefing room. As soon as the officer has put on his uniform shirt with the badge of his authority affixed, the adrenaline flow begins to increase ever-so-slightly. Most likely, not even the officer can clearly detect the increase.

The watch commander, usually a sergeant, but sometimes a lieutenant, sits at the head of the table surrounded by those on the shift. The watch commander reads a briefing board reporting those things that need special attention, such as activities requested to be followed up by the detectives or other shift watch commanders. Areas of patrol assignments are made as well as the vehicles to be used for the shift. Depending on the identifying number of the squad car such as 2-P-10, that same number will be the identifying nomenclature the deputy is assigned to and the car will be used to identify himself on the police radio. As soon as the deputy has all of his personal effects placed into the car, the shotgun rack is unlocked, the gun removed, unloaded, checked, reloaded, then returned to the locked shotgun rack. The officer reports to the dispatcher that he is en route to his assigned patrol area. Once more that life-saving adrenaline again begins to, ever-so-slowly, increase. The graveyard shift has hit the streets.

From midnight to 0200 are the hours that the streets are usually still moving with the bright headlights, from mostly cars flashing in the one direction and the red taillights flashing about in the other direction, giving the darkness an eerie and sometimes grotesque mingling of flashing, multi-colored neon lights of businesses with the haze of street lights. The excitement of the night to come is highlighted with this manmade Aurora Borealis of dancing hews.

At 2:00 a.m., the bars close down; therefore, the restaurant's alcohol drinks stop flowing. Now the streets are less filled with the kind of traffic that started the morning. Most of the business lights are dimmed, but not all. Mixed with a small amount of employees returning home from their late night shift are the cars returning from the bars.

When graveyard begins and when the day darkens, many peace officers fall or are killed in the course of their job to protect the public while you are in your home safe. The hunt begins for criminals, and we find them with handguns, knives, and all kinds of weapons. This is the time the drug addict's dope is taken, and in any given time, there is probably over a ton of dope taken daily through this nation. As you slide under your warm blankets, that cop is working the graveyard shift. Sleep peacefully and remember the road warriors are chasing crooks out in the neighborhood.

The night gets really active at this time with husbands and wives getting home from partying.

Soon the domestic violence and disturbance calls will start. The drunk drivers are on the street, attempting to make it home before they get caught in a car stop by some police officer. The adrenaline begins to flow stronger as the officer listens intently to hear the radio blurt out his specific unit call sign as his head swivels from left to right, eyes darting into the rear-view mirror all the while watching the traffic and street ahead. Compared with a typical night battling with the enemy, the violent drunks, some Chicago-like punks with guns who think very little of life, the paranoid who has been up for days looking for his next score, and those willing to kill a cop to keep their speed or heroin.

The graveyard shift has begun.

I began hundreds of graveyard shifts in this familiar way.

I recently finished a twenty-nine-year run with the San Bernardino County Sheriff Department. It was an exhausting period. I was fortunate to be able to work with so many talented people coupled with a job that was very challenging. As I went through the ranks, I did my best to rid the county communities of the criminals that preyed on the innocent. This county is the largest in America and is 20,000 miles, almost bigger than Rhode Island, and most of the county is made up of desert and mountains and there are several charted cities within the county. Most of these cities are covered most with the protection of the San Bernardino County Sheriff as their police law enforcement, local traffic, issues, and crime and the Highway Patrol covers the interstate freeways. The department also has its own identification division which includes CSI responsibilities. Homicide, crimes against children, its own press corps, and the large horse mounted posse works closely with search teams and mine rescue team trackers. From the top to the bottom, from sheriff to all the support personnel, everyone did all they could to protect the street cops. One of the most important positions protecting the backs of the officers was the dispatchers. The stress of that job also takes its devastating toll. I never worked with a dispatcher who did not suffer from the effects of the overwhelming stress involved in listening for the safety of the officer the dispatcher was responsible to protect. Of all the positions in law enforcement, the dispatcher is one of the most respected and admired by all.

The sheriff is also responsible for the operations of the largest low-rise jail in the country. The building barely fits in sixty acres. The jail houses several thousand prisoners and has the most advanced electronics. If the operation finds itself in an emergency situation, there is a deputy called the control master deputy who will push a button and it will activate all the doors leading to the outside of the facility as well as all the doors in prisoner housing buildings. I helped design the building while I was working with Deputy Chief Lenny Johnson. I considered Deputy Chief Johnson as a genius in jail operations. It was an honor to work in that enormous project with this brilliant man for I learned much from him, and when anything involving law enforcement in this business you must complete work in absolute detail because lives are at stake. There is no room for mistakes when you are dealing with people's lives. The department was very lucky to have him with the department.

Although the experience of being a patrol officer is extremely rewarding, there are also many downsides to the job. For many men and women, law enforcement officers working graveyard shift will have a difficult time getting good, restful sleep and spending quality time with the family. Usually their brains are still going one hundred miles per hour, and their body wants to rest. It is difficult when you spent the last eight hours racing to the next call. Typical of this is knowing the next graveyard shift is going to be a long eight hours because you must be in court to testify on the arrest you made a couple of days ago when you hooked and booked someone for drunk driving. You are waiting in the hall of the courthouse reviewing your notes of the arrest before you are called in the courtroom and notified it is your time to testify. Then you finally get to go home, and as you change in the locker room, slip out of your uniform in to your street clothing, you drive home telling yourself you are almost home. Finally, you stagger in the front door thinking in a minute or two, you will slide under the covers and let yourself fall blissfully asleep.

The loss of normal sleep in the law enforcement business in every assignment worked is one of the things which take their greatest toll. This is especially true for the married officers with children. The balancing act of obtaining sufficient sleep and meeting the needs of a wife and needs of those children add to the stress of the job. But it is not so smooth. The wife has a complaint the kids were misbehaving and need to be talked to later. She has a to-do list for you and if you can, you work on that list so you get to go to sleep. And as you doze off, the wife can't vacuum, and the phone rings, and it is a friend who wants conversation. You tell him you will call back because you have to get some sleep. The drip from the faucet keeps getting louder and louder and, for some unknown reason, stops and you think now you can go to sleep. Ah, wonderful sleep and you finally reach a deep sleep when the door opens suddenly and you jump out of bed, wondering why the SWAT is in your house, and then you hear your son saying his brother has his baseball and won't give it back. You call your other son and tell him to give the baseball back, and he says he doesn't have it.

"Then why is he saying you have it?" You plead with the wife to take care of the problem. The infant girl is crying, and you beg for the noise to stop. For many people working the graveyard shift, they lose a little sleep and try to spend quality time with the family also. The whole family is trying to juggle the schedule during the day. We all love it though and like a fickle girlfriend, hate it at the same time.

Court Hearings and Testifying

One of the peace officer's important duties is to testify. You must appear in court as you are required to tell about the arrest. If the judge decides there is enough information to hold a complete court hearing, a jury will be selected from the population. At this hearing, the defendant's attorney or court-appointed defense attorney will defend the defendant for free. The whole process begins when the attorneys select the jurors. The jurors will listen to the evidence and weigh the information so they can be relied on to give the court a verdict. This process continues until the jury is ready to give a verdict about whether the defendant is guilty or innocent.

The officer must attend the entire hearing. Some hearings last a short time, and some can go on for many months. The graveyard officer is the one who suffers from the loss and the officer must deal with this situation as best as he can. There are certain techniques you can use during a court hearing.

Make sure you follow these simple procedures:

1. When you speak, make sure you are speaking loud enough so everyone can hear you.

2. When you speak, look directly at the attorney and, when it is possible, look at the jury.

3. Do not show anger while you are testifying. When you do that, the jury may believe that you have a personal vendetta against the defendant.

4. When attending the court hearing, wear professional clothing. At a court hearing, the judge threw out a defense attorney because he was dressed in Levi's and wasn't wearing a tie.

5. Do not chew any gum.

6. Only answer questions that are given to you.

7. Don't volunteer anything, or you will look like you are anxious to hang the defendant. Remember, the district attorney is going to be nice to you, but the defense attorney will go after you and try to trip you up

8. Do not ever talk to jurors outside the court room. That will cause a mistrial.

Follow these general rules:

1. Tape-record your interview. You don't get to ask questions before you give the suspect his rights.

2. If the suspect volunteers a statement, you can use it in court. These statements are considered spontaneous statements.

3. If you have two or more prisoners in the back seat, turn on the recorder and make a recording of their conversations. You have a good likelihood of getting an admission from this conversation from one or more of them, and it can be used in court. Just tell them you will be leaving them alone for a minute. I was able to find out where they hid the weapon used in a robbery when one of the prisoners said, "I hope he doesn't look in the bushes."

4. It is important to have good fingerprints when the defendant is booked in the local jail.

5. Don't forget to search your prisoner before you take him inside the jail. I remember searching a prisoner the highway patrol brought in the search and uncuff room. This is one of the first rooms you enter when you bring in a prisoner. When I searched him I found a 0.25 caliber handgun in the suspect's back pocket. The officer was lucky because they drove around the area for a while before they brought the prisoner in for booking for a DWI. They were lucky on that graveyard shift.

6. Once you fall into a large investigation where multiple witnesses are involved, it is your responsibility to keep in touch with the witnesses until the court hearing. The district attorney will be in contact with the witnesses and will request the witnesses come to his office one by one and he will talk to them to discuss the entire case.

7. As you are working graveyard, when it is a slow morning, get yourself a large cup of coffee someplace where you are visible to the public and study your reports. Remember, you must be on the move checking industrial buildings in your beat as well as retail stores. These areas will be most likely attacked by burglars.

8. A smart patrolman will plan his night, including the calls that come in for service. There are nights that will be nonstop, and you do the best you can and hope you have prepared enough for the court hearing. Several officers did not go home and stayed at the station reviewing reports until they were 100 percent ready. After the court hearing, you go straight home and collapse and hope the wife or girlfriend is cooperative and lets you sleep until you must get ready for the next graveyard shift. On many occasions

when you report to briefing, you are told there are many calls left for you to handle from swing shift. That means swing shift was very busy and sometimes calls stack up. When you notify the dispatcher you are 10-8, it means you are ready to take the first call.

If you follow these rules, you will be a winner. I have never lost a case, and I am very proud of that. I've had some close calls but I ended up winning because I did a thorough job and the other officers on the case did an outstanding job including the lab SID.

CHAPTER 1

After the Robbery

We all heard the help request. Once we got to the location, we all responded and got the suspect's information for an all-points bulletin broadcast. As I stepped out of an unmarked unit, a deputy exiting the store ran up to me and said "We have a bad scene here, and the clerk is badly shaken and unable to talk to us."

I replied to the deputy, "What do you mean she is unable to talk to us? She has to talk to us. We need the suspect's information." I asked the deputy if she was injured and if she has any wounds? He replied no. "Then for Pete's sakes what is going on around here? I will talk to her." I walked into the store and found her crouched behind the counter shaking. I asked her to walk with me, and she stood up. I grabbed her hand and told her she was safe because the deputies are here now. "Tell me what happened. What did the men look like, and did you happen to see the car?"

She said, "There were two men wearing ski masks, but I think the guy with the shotgun had a mustache and the taller one, he put the shotgun to my head and said "When I pull the trigger it would take a second and then you will blackout. Then the shorter of the two suspects talked to the man with the shotgun, he pleaded with him not to shoot me. And he said, 'I have to kill you!' Then he pressed the gun back against my head. I pleaded with him, 'Please don't kill me, I have a baby at home, and she needs me.' The he shoved the front of the shotgun at me, and after that, they emptied the cash drawer and left in the dark. A few seconds later, the deputy arrived."

I asked her what they were wearing.

She told me both men were wearing black windbreaker jackets with white lettering on the back. "I don't remember what it spelled."

I asked "Did the other guy have a gun?"

She replied "Yes, he did."

I went to my car radio and gave the description over the air for all responding units, then I advised them to respond to the other stores just in case they hit another one. I warned them that they are armed with a shotgun and a handgun, and according to the victim, the guy with the shotgun is the most dangerous. I told the deputy to do a good crime investigation and not to forget to dust for prints and nominally do the crime scene.

As I got in my car, suddenly I heard a deputy yelling. He has been shot by the suspects at another 7-Eleven store. The two suspects had left that store, and there was a gunfight. The deputy said he was shot in the foot. All the units were told to get to the onramps on the freeway and respond to the location of the shooting.

I met with Deputy K J Johnson, and he was not wounded after all. It looks like one pellet from the shotgun blast hit him in shoe. Johnson gave a better description of the suspects. There were two white males, one with a mustache. He gave a good description of the taller one who took the mask off as he jumped a wall while the other suspect headed to his car and left the scene at a high speed. Shortly, a police unit spotted the car. One of our units was with the Colton officer, and they got the shorter of the suspects, Cal. After another officer stopped that suspect who drove away on the freeway and arrested him in Colton, I took the suspect with me to the station and started questioning him. I asked him what his last name was, and he would not give any information. About the second suspect, I ran a DMV check of the vehicle, and it came back belonging to Fred Baker out of Riverside, California. I advised the watch commander that I would be going to Riverside for follow-up. Meanwhile, I asked if a deputy could take the robbery suspect to the hospital for the wound to his chest. Cal was shot in the chest area. He said he was shot by his partner as they drove to Riverside. It was about a half-hour drive. I asked Cal how he got shot. He was reaching for the car door to open it and that maniac shot him in the chest and he said Jack did it because he did not want to leave a witness, including me. I asked him what is Jack's last name, and he replied Maniac.

I subsequently made contact with Mr. Baker. He was not the second suspect. I advised him his car was used in a robbery, and he said it couldn't be because it was here all night, and he pointed to a blue Ford. He told me he had sold the car to a guy named Jack Maniac. He continued telling me the buyer lived in the Riverside area. I requested the Fontana dispatcher notify the Riverside Sheriff to respond to my location. In a few minutes I asked the sheriff if he had any information on Maniac. When he ran the license plate, it came back that the car was reported as stolen. I told the officer that I would take the report since the car was used in an armed robbery. I also would have to interview the reporting party and needed to talk to her for my investigation. I further told the officer I would meet with him in the morning before the end of this shift. He agreed. I thanked him then left and proceeded up the street to the address of the reporting party.

The address was in a trailer park. I found the address inside the trailer park in Space X at the front of the park. I pulled in front of the trailer. It was a cold freezing, windy morning as I walked up to the front door and knocked several times. Finally the door opened, and an attractive woman answered the door. I told her I was there to take a stolen car report. The wind kept blowing my paper making it impossible for me to write anything down. I suggested to her that I be allowed inside the trailer. I told her I really had work to do, and the wind kept me from writing down my notes. She was wearing a robe and was hesitant at first, then agreed. She stepped aside, allowing me to come in. So I stepped inside, and once I got inside, she told me I would have to be quick because she had to go to work soon. I asked her if she was married, and she replied yes. I asked her where her husband was, and she told me he was sleeping in the bedroom. I told her to go and get him and she said no to me.

I said, "What do you mean?" I told her I was investigating a serious crime and told her that if she was not going to go get him, then I will do it. Then she complied, and she walked down a hallway to the back of the trailer.

I sat on a bar stool next to the kitchen counter. A short time later, I could hear the shower running. She finally came back to my location without the husband. I asked her where the husband was, and she told me he was taking a shower. She knew that I was annoyed, and I told her then I had no time to play games with her and as soon as I told her that he walked out of the hallway. His arms were full of jailhouse tattoos and he had a lightning bolt on the side of his neck, and a tear dropped under his left eye. As soon as I saw him, I knew he was going to be trouble. He was one of the biggest dirt bags I have seen with prison tattoos on his face and neck. I was certain he was my second suspect. As he walked into the kitchen, he stepped behind the counter. I noticed he had shaved his mustache off, and there were blood droplets above his upper lip. At first I thought he didn't match with her, she was very neat and well groomed.

I did not make my move yet, I wanted him to talk some more. I told him I was investigating the report of the stolen car and needed to go back to my car and get my notebook. I left the trailer to go to the car and when I got to the car I racked a round in the chamber of the gun just in case.

When I walked back in, he walked up to the counter and was standing behind it and facing me. When I asked him when he discovered the car was missing, he said 1:30 a.m. Then he reached in and pulled out a pack of cigarettes from his shirt pocket. When he pulled out the pack, along with the pack came tumbling out one Ontario police traffic citation. The ticket fell out of his pocket and landed in front of me. He reached for it, however, I picked up the citation, and I got it before he was able to. Then I looked at the ticket, and it listed him as Jack Maniac. He then knew I was on to him. The citation was issued at 2:00 a.m. He told me the car was stolen at 1:30 and it would have been impossible for that car to travel from the city of Ontario to Riverside. I got off the chair and stepped back from the counter and pulled out my handgun from my ankle holster, pointed it at him and said "You are under arrest for armed robbery." I told him to put his hands up and step around the counter into the living room and turn around. He began reaching under the countertop. I told him to lift his hands up or he'll get shot. Then I had him walking into the living room where I handcuffed him. While putting him in handcuffs his wife grabbed my arm and I told her to keep her hands off of me or she was going to jail.

I walked out to my car with him and had her walk out also and placed him in the back seat of the unit. I advised Fontana dispatch that I had a second suspect in custody. This was my first contact with Maniac.

Next I began a draft of the search warrant then jumped in my car and drove back to Riverside. I asked for a back-up deputy to stand by the trailer and prevent anyone from entering the trailer. I needed a judge to approve the search warrant.

Upon arriving back at the trailer Detective O'Campo was there to assist me in the search. I appreciated him being there. He helped me when I was a rookie. O.C. was the first deputy I rode on patrol with and I learned much from him and I was always grateful to him.

After I handed Mary Maniac a copy of the search warrant, we began searching for the shotgun, the black jacket, and anything to tie Maniac to the robberies. I searched the bedroom and I found the jacket in the closet and yes indeed, it was the jacket he was wearing when he committed the robbery. The back of the jacket had white letters reading two words "Moving Company" and that was it, just the lettering. Shortly after I found the jacket, OC called to me and said he found the shotgun, and he tried to pull it out, but it was still jammed. I requested a dispatcher to contact Ontario Police Department and ask if they had any recent robberies.

I went back to the station and transported Maniac and placed him in a cell with Cal.

After meeting with the Riverside officer and giving him his GTA (Grand Theft Auto), I returned to the station to do my paperwork. The following day, I went to the District Attorney's Office and received a first-degree robbery complaint. A jury found him guilty. He was given twenty years.

His partner received twenty years and was sent to Pelican Bay and then transferred to Folsom and later he paroled. Maniac was transferred to Folsom later when he got life without parole. A year later, I received a call from a prison lieutenant, telling me Maniac told another inmate that he wanted to kill me.

Later on the day that Cal had been arrested, and I interviewed him. He stated that several times when Cal shared the same cell with Maniac, he told him that he was trying to kill me. He related the scenario to me. While I was outside, the trailer during the arrest, the husband was trying to pull a shotgun from a tight place under the bottom drawer where he had hidden it. This was the shotgun used in the robberies that morning. I was very lucky that morning that the shotgun was jammed in that space, for as I found out later, he was going to shoot me in the face as soon as I reentered. Once I was shot, he was going to drag me into the trailer and wrap me up with a sheet and keep my body until it got dark, then he was going to drag me out and place me inside my trunk and drive me to Perris Lake in Riverside and get rid of the car and me in the lake. He told Cal he knew a place at the lake that was very deep by the shore. He said nobody would see the car with me inside the trunk.

Cal, the other robber, further told me that while I was sitting writing my notes, Maniac had a camping ax on a shelf on his side of the counter in a place where I couldn't see it and planned to grab the ax and quickly hit me on the head. Just as he was going to do it, I moved my leg, and he saw my gun strapped to my ankle, and he noticed my hand was very close to my handgun, and he was afraid to grab the ax. He felt he would not be able to reach my head, and as soon as he made his move, I would pull out my gun first and shoot him. This information put chills up my arms. I guess it was not my time to die. Cal told me that before they robbed the stores, they both robbed a couple of stores in Ontario. While inside, if they got stopped after robbing the stores, Jack was going to kill any cop as soon as he walked up to the car window. Cal talked him out of it, telling him if you kill a cop, they put you in the gas chamber—plus every cop in the state will be looking for them.

"Look, Danna, that Ontario cop does not know how close he came to being killed last night when he pulled us over after the robbery for the traffic violation. When the officer walked up to the car, Maniac was going to kill him."

There were stories relayed to me by Cal that Maniac had killed before.

One scenario was when Jack and I were in Ontario, and Jack found information for a pickup truck he wanted to buy, so he called the number in the ad, and he told the person he had no car. He asked the seller if it would be okay if he drove the pickup to him in Ontario, and he would test drive it with him, and if he liked it, he would buy it and then take him back to his house. The person agreed, and eventually he arrived. Jack had put a shovel in the back of the bed of the truck, and when he returned with the truck, I asked him, "Where is the guy who owned the truck?"

"I shot him in the face and buried him." Jack told me to help him clean the blood off the dashboard and the seat. Jack started to laugh because he got a good deal on a truck. I asked where he was buried, and he said in wooded area.

I went to the airport and found the area with several reserves, and we searched most of the day. We could not find anything like some freshly dug-up dirt on top of the ground. We came up empty, unless Jack buried the body somewhere else. There were few large trees. I would not call it a wooded area; there was a lot of brush in this area to the west of the runway near a fence. I checked with the airport about any reports of a found body. The story could not be verified.

Couple shot

Cal said a couple owed his mom money for rent. They were from Fontana. He went into their house when they were sleeping, went into the bedroom, and shot them both with a shotgun while they were in bed. After he killed them, a baby started crying in a crib. Jack said he was going to kill the baby. Instead, he grabbed the baby and threw it onto the dead bodies, and the baby stopped crying so he left. He had warned those people that they better come up with some money, or they will pay.

Hooker Murdered

Maniac bragged about the day he and a friend picked up a hooker in Ontario from the truck stop. They were smoking some dope, and Jack started talking about killing someone in Riverside.

Jack realized the hooker overheard the story about the couple with the baby he killed and decided to kill her because she listened that made her a potential witness against him. She was very unlucky. So Jack grabbed and choked the hooker and forced a whole bag of reds and barbiturates down her throat so the cops would think she overdosed. Then he and his friend dragged the body in the shower and washed down any evidence like DNA, etc. Jack said he sodomized her. Then both of them carried her to his

friend's station wagon, and they drove to North Fontana. Jack came up with the idea of driving at a fast rate of speed up a dirt road. Then he would slide her so she was face down and hands down out of the station wagon. When her face hits the ground it would rub off, and so would her fingertips. During graveyard shift in morning, a friend drove Maniac while he held her from the back of the wagon holding on to her feet while she was facedown, and they did it until the car hit a bump, causing Jack to lose his grip as she fell onto the road.

The next morning, the body was found by a jogger. I went to the local Fontana police department responsible and gave them the information. What did they do with the information, I don't know. All that he bragged about was not in done in their county. There is no proof of any of this. I will never know, but I do know Jack is crazy enough he may have done all these things.

A judge had been convinced to allow Jack to be at home under his mother's supervision because of crowded conditions. He was under house arrest at her apartment. She was the manager of a complex.

Maniac's mother told Jack days later to give her a hand and go collect the late rent from one resident. So Jack went to the apartment to collect money. When he made contact with the renter, the man told him he had no money. That was the wrong thing to say to Jack. When the guy refused him, Jack pulled out a gun and shot and killed him right at the door in front of witnesses. They called 911.

When the police arrived, Jack was hiding in the attic of the victim's apartment. The police pulled him out at gunpoint and eventually forced him down and arrested him with no further incident.

The judge paid for his stupid decision to allow Maniac out of jail on bail against the district attorney's advice and suffered the consequence. Of course, when we found out what the judge did, the public went crazy, and everyone wanted the judge thrown off the bench before he could fix his blunder. When election time came around, the people threw a rally against the judge and forced him out.

There is no doubt in my mind that Maniac must stay in prison for the rest of his miserable life because he is a major danger to the public.

He was found guilty of first degree murder, and he ended up being transported to Pelican Bay—one of the toughest prisons in America—with a life sentence. He is still doing time but was later transferred to Folsom.

I am retired now, and this information only demonstrates there are people out there that are very dangerous. If you are not careful, you could be a victim someday. At least we have professional police officers, and we have a great court system.

Amboy Volcano

In one of the areas in San Bernardino County, there is a place called Amboy with a population of about five people. One restaurant in Amboy has been used in several commercials. It was intended to give you a feeling that you are out in the middle of nowhere. As a deputy chief of the region, I had very remote areas I was responsible for. This small desert town in the high desert has a very small volcano within the town limits (outskirts of town). The last time the volcano erupted was ten thousand years ago. It has been said that the last time it went off, the desert was a lush green.

There is a story about this volcano and an old prospector who lived in the outskirts of the town named Jake. One day, the old desert rat decided to take a bunch of old tires from the gas station in town, and Old Jake decided to clean up the town because it was so near the freeway the town was full of old discarded tires. Jake looked around and couldn't find a place to get rid of all the tires, so one day, he thought to himself why not take all these tires and throw them into the volcano. So as the legend goes, Old Jake began the task of hauling the old tires off to the volcano. He took his mule to carry all these tires, and it took him weeks to finish the job. Now Old Jake decided to bum all of these tires one day, and he climbed back up to the volcano with two cans of gasoline. Jake threw the gasoline onto the tires and lit a match to set the tires on fire. The fire became large with flames and thick with black smoke, and at night, there was a glow of red. People driving by Amboy thought the volcano was erupting again so they called the police to report the eruption.

The sheriff responded along with the fire department, and the sheriff contacted the CHP. The CHP responded and was planning to close down Interstate 15, the route to Las Vegas, for public safety. When the casino moguls in Las Vegas heard of the potential closing of the road, and they went ballistic and demanded the road be opened immediately before they lost millions. The CHP refused until the governor got involved. The moguls made contact with the governor of Nevada to request the military do something and have the National Guard activated using their firefighting planes to drop water into the cone and put out the eruption. The experts informed them they cannot do that because it can cause an explosion, and you can't turn off a volcano like that.

The five people in the town said Old Jake got in trouble, so he got two buckets filled with water and carried them up to the volcano, and it took him about a hundred trips to put the fire out. As Jake was putting the slow-burning fire out, and every time he threw water on the burning tires, the smoke changed color, turning it to light gray. Old Jake knew he stirred up a hornet's nest, so he got out of town as soon as he could get his old yellow Javelin Plymouth fixed, and he drove that clunker into the desert. He has not been seen since, and the moguls were happy.

Because the crisis was over, they did not lose any money. Some people heard this story and believed that is why the Mirage Hotel placed a volcano in front of their casino.

Now this story has been passed down for many years. Was it true? I have never researched it. Mr. Winn decided to build his volcano in front of one of his casinos on the strip. So when the visitors go to the strip, they can see his volcano erupt about every twenty minutes. Yep, if you happen to drive past the Mirage Hotel Casino and see their volcano going they might be burning old tires. It is just a guess, but I heard Jake is now a big mogul and now some people believe Old Jake is really Nick the Greek. Is this story folklore? I really can't say if it is true or not. You decide.

I can tell you that many years later, there was a creep sweep in Amboy. The descendants of those original five people were arrested. Sergeant Winstead and I conducted a criminal sweep in the town. We descended on the town of Amboy and raided a meth lab seizing two pounds of processed speed. After that. he and his deputies were through the town it almost became a ghost town. I eventually drove to Amboy to meet Lloyd. It was there late on graveyard shift, and he advised me that he and the deputies found a large lab processing operation in the town. Later, it was found that the suspects were making many thousands of dollars, and he further told me he had several suspects in custody at gun point. He caught them in the process of cooking the meth. This illegal drug is very dangerous and puts poison gas in the air. If you inhale too much of it, the gas can kill you, and it is highly explosive.

He arrested all five people living in the town, and one person was left. We took in all five and left Amboy a ghost town. The only person left in town was Jake; the rest lived in Amboy went to jail for outstanding warrants. We went to the town, and Sergeant Winstead came with me to talk with these people who told Winstead these descendants swear they see Old Jake when there is a full moon standing on top of the volcano. Three months later, the town was placed on sale.

There is another small town called Newberry Springs, and I set up a raid in that area. Both Winstead and I took some people out of a house at gunpoint for manufacturing the drug methamphetamine. In this line of work, they are called cookers. We seized one pound and set up another sweep in another dot on the map in a town called Trona. Now there is a resident deputy who lives in Trona, and one deputy is the entire law enforcement for this small desert town. You can smell the town.

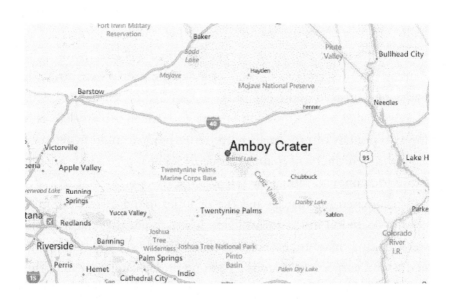

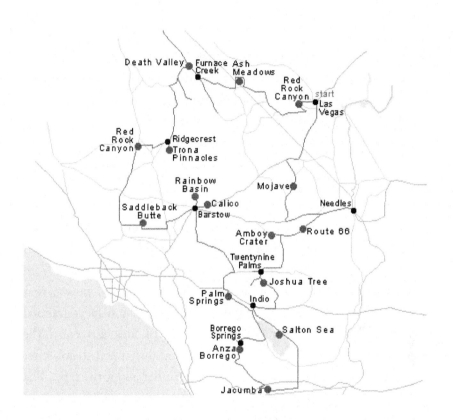

Attempted Murder and Rape

I received a call to respond to a location in a very isolated area where Riverside County borders San Bernardino County. The counties meet by a small dam called Prado Dam. The dam is located there to resolve flooding conditions occurring during the rainy season.

It was a nearby location of an attempted rape and murder. When I arrived at the location and as I closed in on the area, I noticed the flashing red and blue emergency lights of a highway patrol's unit. They were waiting with a female victim in their patrol car and advised me they called the paramedics to take a look at the victim as she was beaten really badly. I shined my flashlight into the unit, and they were right she was bruised all over. Her face was swollen from the beating, and she was injured extensively from the person that tried to rape her. As she was jogging in the area, the suspect grabbed her and dragged her off in the weeds and brush area adjacent to the dam. I took her off the hands of the CHP and thanked them. After placing her in my unit, I started to question her about the rape. The CHP wasted no time going back on the freeway with knowledge they owed me a supplemental report of what their involvement was, finding the victim, etc. Based on the victim's description, the attack happened on the San Bernardino County's side, and it was our rape for sure.

I interviewed the victim, and she told me the following: She decided to take a late night run. Usually she runs ten miles to the dam, and then returns back home. She was running by the dam, and a man jumped out of the bushes and grabbed her, knocking her down and grabbed her by the hair. She described the man as a very short man, and he was very strong. He pulled up her sweatshirt over her head and exposed her breasts, then he placed her mouth over her nipples, biting them. Then he pulled down her sweatpants and underwear and pulled his pants down and tried to enter her. She continued struggling as he began choking her. He stopped when she played dead because he thought he killed her. The suspect grabbed her face and shook it, believing she was dead and said "Oh shit!" He panicked and began cursing himself, saying, "Oh please, don't die. And he said, "I have to get rid of her." Then he grabbed her by the ankles and dragged her toward his car and opened his car trunk.

"I guess I was too heavy for him, and he dropped me to the ground. I was going to put up a fight, but I didn't and continued to play dead. I think it saved my life." she said. I agreed with her and told her she did well. She told me he was like a crazy man, and when he was punching her, he kept yelling, "You dirty bitch" over and over again and began choking her. He was unsuccessful getting her into the trunk because he was unable to lift her off the ground high enough. After several attempts, he gave up and dragged her farther into the brush. She described him as having strong hands for a little man. She knew that if he was successful in getting her in the trunk, she would have no chance of survival. She continued to play dead, and he actually thought she was dead, and she heard him say to himself.

"Please don't die here." Then after several minutes, he threw some branches over her and he left, driving away. The victim said she lay motionless until she thought he was gone for sure.

She told me, "I waited several minutes, then I ran to the side of the freeway and waved my arms for a car to stop and help me. I was very lucky to get the CHP and heard them call for you guys."

She had some serious bruises on her neck. She asked me if I wanted to see the teeth marks on her breasts. I told her I would have a female deputy look. I asked her if she had any additional information about the suspect who attacked her. She said when he was trying to get her in his trunk, she noticed very colorful clothing in there, and she was able to see the clothing when the lights went on in the trunk, illuminating it inside. She described the car as being older and large.

I waited for the paramedics to arrive and asked her if she would be able to identify him and could she describe him. I told her after the interview was finished, I will have the sheriff dispatcher make the calls to the identification division and meet me at the station for a composite. We would make a composite of him and a flyer, and the flyer will be sent to all California law enforcement agencies. The ambulance arrived, and the medics looked at her. I told them to take her to the hospital and that I wanted a rape examination done. I told her I would meet her at the hospital and asked her if she wanted her relatives to meet her at the hospital. She asked me to call her boyfriend to come to the hospital and pick her up. She was transported to the nearest hospital. I arrived before the ambulance and shortly after that the ambulance pulled in and walked her inside. In the full light, boy, he really roughed her up badly. I could see deep red marks on both sides of her neck where he placed his hands to choke her.

I went to the station, and based on her description, I thought the suspect might be a jockey——short with strong hands. Jockeys need strong hands to handle the reins of a horse. I felt concerned about the case because the suspect was trying to kill her. This guy was very dangerous and needed to be caught as soon as possible. I knew I was going with the composite to the Hollywood Race Track in Santa Anita and hoped she could give a good description of the suspect, so it was very important for me and my fingers were crossed for a little luck. I knew it was difficult to get a good composite from a victim, especially one who went through trauma I was very happy with my victim. She was very intelligent and gave the tech an excellent description that was very detailed. She told us he would have four deep scratches on his cheeks. When she said that, I knew I would have to go the next day before those scratches healed. I did not ask the sergeant if I could work my day off because they were trying to keep overtime down. I did not want to take a chance of being turned down. I wanted to get this in the notes that he tried to kill her.

The next day, I went to the Hollywood Race Track and met with the groundskeeper and showed him the composite. I figured he knew every jockey. He identified the picture right away and told me the jockey was not at the facility that day and told me he had called in sick and was not coming in to work. He was supposed to run some trials and run some horses for time on the track. The groundskeeper offered a photograph. The photograph was very close to the composite. I asked him to keep quiet, and if the jockey comes in to work tomorrow, to look at his cheeks to see if he has scratches and call me. I told him to be quiet about this, and he asked me if there was a reward. I told him I was sorry there was none, except he would be helping the sheriff department and not to say anything to anyone. I went to the station and ordered a Soundex, which is a copy of his driver's license and photograph lineup. Then I requested look-a-likes of him.

The next day, I went to the Los Angeles County Fairgrounds and met with the person who was responsible for the jockeys at the fair. I lucked out. He had color photographs of the jockeys on his office wall. I requested all the photographs on the wall, and he pulled a book off a shelf and opened the book. The book had four more photographs of the jockeys that raced at the track for media and publicity purposes. I asked him if all of the jockeys still race at the track, and he pulled out two pictures and said one of the jockeys left abruptly. He did not know why or where he went.

I wanted to see if the photos matched any mug pictures taken at the jail by the arresting officer during an arrest. The mug shots are two and a half inches long by two inches wide. The manager told me that there are four races at the county fair racetrack regularly. I asked him to keep quiet about my visit. I explained why I needed the photos, and he told me he would cooperate. He assured me he would note I took possession of the photographs and to let him know if I needed future assistance from him. I left as soon as possible to get back to the station so I could call the victim to come in and look at some pictures.

When I got back to the station, I pulled out a box filled with mug photos and placed them on a photo lineup card. This card holds eight photographs. I placed the pictures of the jockeys into the spaces of the seven by eleven card with six or seven open sections. The spaces are for the officer to place mug photographs in each section, and it came out great. I placed a photograph of the suspect in the number 5 slot and hoped she would say that number.

I requested the victim come to the station and look at some pictures. When she met with me, I explained to her that I was going to show a group of pictures to her, and the attacker may be one in the series. I explained that when she looks at the pictures and sees the suspect in one of the slots, to tell me what the number is under the picture. Then I gave her the lineup card of the pictures. The victim looked and appeared stunned and dropped the photo lineup on the floor and let out a sigh and said, "Yes, the man in this picture." I asked her if she was absolutely sure. She said, "Yes, this is the guy who tried to kill me."

I made a copy of the lineup and had her place her initials under the photograph she selected. "That was all that I wanted, and now I am going after him." I told her and thanked her and let her go home. After she left, I advised the sergeant what occurred and that I was going to the district attorney to get a criminal complaint for the suspect. I took my report to District Attorney Jim Faust, and he was satisfied and drew up the complaint.

I took the paperwork to Superior Court for an arrest warrant and asked for a $100,000 warrant good for both night and day service. The judge signed the warrant off, and I went directly to the race track to get the suspect into custody. I wanted to contact the groundskeeper at the race track. He said the guy never reported in, and he was gone when I got there. I just missed him and was told by the track manager that Jack left, complaining he did not feel good so he drove home sick. When I arrived at his home, I got there just in time to catch him backing out of a parking space. I blocked the car and jumped out of my car. I pulled him out of his car at gunpoint. He was so afraid, he wet his trousers because I scared him so much with the gun barrel screwed in his ear.

Later he told me he thought I was an IRS agent because he owed back taxes. I told him I guess owing back taxes to the government is more serious to him than attempted murder and rape.

I transported him to the station for interviewing and placed him in the interview room and called the victim. However, her father answered, and once he knew I had the suspect in custody, he replied that his daughter did not want to testify. I told the father to please understand and explained "We need to put this guy in prison." He agreed. I told him I would come over and talk to his daughter and try to convince her everything would be all right and to further explain to her there is no case without her testimony, and I needed her full cooperation. That is when the father dropped the bomb. He said he sent her to Europe for a long vacation. I told him I was very sorry for the decision they made.

I got this dirt bag out of the room and drove him back to his home. I threatened him all the way home telling him I was going to get him one day. He better move to some other state or some other planet because I am going to watch him for a long time. I was going to check with every city and town police departments within two hundred miles from the race track and ask if they had any unsolved violent rape by a suspect that looked like a munchkin.

Rape by Moonlight

It was a bright night with a full moon. I was struggling to keep my eyes open because instead of getting sleep before I reported to work, I had to be in court most of the day as the investigating officer for one of my cases. I still had several hours to go on graveyard, and it was three in the morning. I was exhausted as I headed to Los Serranos, a low-income residential area.

This area was normally very dark due to lack of street lights. But tonight, it was bright thanks to the full moon. I saw some movement ahead stopped driving in the middle of the street and pulled to the side of the deserted street. I could easily make out it was a naked female. Suddenly I see a beautiful naked blonde female approaching me. I stepped out of my patrol car, and as soon as I was out of the car, I could hear her yelling, "Help me, I have been raped." She came closer, and I walked toward her. She grabbed me in a bear hug and almost knocked me over. She was crying and pleading for me to help her. I opened the car door and grabbed a blanket and put it around her and put my jacket around her and placed her in the unit. I finally calmed her down. I told her she was safe now and asked, "Where did this happen?" She told me where the rape took place. She named her attackers, and I knew them all. She told me it happened in the backyard of a vacant house. I knew where this vacant house was.

I advised dispatch. I needed a reserve patrol car and told them I have a rape victim with me. When the backup reserve unit arrived, I

46

requested they take the victim to the hospital for a rape examination. I asked them not to question her about the rape, that I would interview her when I got to the station. I explained to the two reserves that we all must be very sensitive to her—the poor girl went through hell. I took her out of my car and transferred the female to their unit. I asked them to transport her to a hospital for an examination where they would collect valuable evidence for pubic hair, semen, etc., for DNA comparison. I warned them not to allow her to go to the bathroom before the examination.

I drove my car to the vacant house. When I approached the house, one of the suspects was walking from the house. When he spotted me, he began running away. I drove the car right behind him then bailed out of the car and ran after him. I threw my Kel-lite and hit him on the back of the head, and down he went. I got him one block away. He stopped struggling when I pinched his midsection, knocking the wind out of him. I placed the handcuffs on him and told him he was under arrest for rape. I threw him into the back seat of the patrol car.

I found the rest of them, and at gunpoint, I had them lay on the ground. I patted them down for any weapons. There were no weapons, and then I stuffed them into the back seat of the unit. I had another deputy help me transport them to the station to complete my investigation and also to the hospital to get a rape kit on them. The other deputy arrived at my location as I pulled them one by one, searched them, and handcuffed them. All these morons, I knew from past contacts.

I booked them all for rape and spent the rest of the night interviewing the victim.

She did well considering what she went through. I called a team to come to the station for I had a rape victim. This is a group of trained volunteers, sometimes known as the God Squad, and they stay with the victim until the victims feel better. They will take her home and take her someplace to eat if she is hungry. They are good listeners. They are good people, and while they had the victim, I went back to the crime scene.

I went back to the house and into the backyard where the rape occurred to look for evidence. While I did the crime scene investigation, I found her blouse, pink shorts, and underwear. I placed them into a bag. I found shoe sole impressions where she explained the actual sex acts happened by two bushes near the fence. I took one-by-one photographs. One-by-one is a technique to get the exact size of the soles from a pair of footwear. I could compare the impressions with the footwear of the suspects, and when I find out who was wearing the boots, I would be able to prove that he participated in the attack. It is a method used for identification and will verify her testimony. Those sole impressions were Vibrant soles. The impressions told me that they were men's work boots. I took photographs of the backyard and questioned the neighbors then left the scene to go to the station.

I was dead tired when I spent several hours interviewing her. It is tough for a man to talk to the female because men recently attacked her. I tried to be as sensitive and compassionate, as it was very difficult to interview a rape victim, especially when it was a vicious gang rape, and she had gone through a terrible attack. She told me in graphic detail about the rape, knew the suspects' names, and when she told me who they were, I also knew them. I finished the paperwork. I had to complete it before I went home because I was off the next day.

The next day, the evidence was tagged for the property room. I placed a rush on the photos so the crime lab could compare the photos of the soles on the footwear with the footwear of the suspects that I knew would match up with the two work boots that had vibrant soles.

The victim moved away. She wrote me a letter, telling me she could not testify. She was very afraid of the suspects' "friends" and what they would do to if she moved back to her mother's home. She thanked me for all the work I did. I did not blame her and totally understood. I can understand her fear of retaliation.

All that work for nothing. I guess this is something that goes with the business—we cannot protect them, and it's a resource issue.

Yes, it's that old moon again. Now don't get me wrong, rapes also occur without the moon in full phase.

Moon Madness

The rain was coming down hard to the extent my windshield wipers were useless. There was loud lighting and the whole nine yards when I received a call very near my location. As I was slowly cruising through the streets in this neighborhood, I was assigned to a family disturbance call near the end of my shift. It took less than a minute to get to the scene. When I arrived at the residence, there were several people in the street pointing at one of the houses. I pulled in the driveway and got out into the rain, and I heard a hysterical woman screaming. Even the loud noise of the rain coming down so hard didn't drown out the sound of her screams. She was yelling for help. I ran up to the opened front door of the house, and when I looked in, I was shocked to see this asshole—a big guy—sitting on top of her, punching her in the face and punching the daylights out of her. He had her pinned down, and I was sure if he continued to punch her, she would surely die. He was completely out of control. I yelled for him to get off of her. He ignored me and yelled back at me to get out the hell out of his house, and he kept on punching her. I ran up to him and wrapped my arm around his neck and tried to pull him off her, but the SOB was not budging, so I stepped back and ran up to him and gave him a hard kick in the face with my size eleven boot—and that kick in the face did the trick. He fell backwards, and the blow dazed him long enough for me to put the handcuffs on him.

I calmed the woman down. Her face was all bloody. I radioed in and requested an ambulance to transport her to the hospital.

He started screaming that I had broken his nose. I grabbed the dope under the armpits and dragged the jerk outside to my patrol car. One of the bystanders ran up to me and offered to help me place the suspect in the car. One by one, the bystanders offered help. The crowd standing by started to clap. I was transporting the idiot to the hospital myself. After the suspect was placed in the car, on the back seat, he tried to kick the window out, I grabbed his nose and twisted it and told him to stop kicking the windows or I will break his nose again. Then he settled down, and when the ambulance arrived for the female, and when I was starting to drive away he spit at me. The spit landed on my collar. I told him to knock it off, and he did it again. I pulled to the curb, stopped and popped open the trunk, pulled him out, and dragged him into the trunk and told him to get in then grabbed his head and pushed once until his head hit the bottom of trunk. His right shoulder fell in, and then I grabbed his legs and threw him in there pushing him down so I could see the trunk door. That is when he started to cry for me to let him out, or he would suffocate. I opened the trunk door and asked him if he was going to spit again. He agreed there would be no more spitting. I felt he thought I was crazy enough to drive while he was in the trunk. When I returned him to the back seat, he remained quiet for the rest of the trip to the hospital. We are required to have the prisoner with an injury checked before the jailer would accept the prisoner. We have to present a hospital clearance for booking.

When I arrived at the hospital, I entered the section that has an entrance for police only, and we walked into a small room several feet from the ER section which was very busy at that time of night. We walked into a waiting room, and the suspect began complaining that the handcuffs were too tight, and he was hurting, so I loosened them. But kept them on him. I looked toward the ER and watched a stocky nurse coming toward me. I was happy, and it looked like I was next. Then Godzilla the nurse came in the room and demanded I take the handcuffs off him. I told her, no, I would not do it because it is against department policy. She said if I did not comply, I could take him to another hospital. So rather than argue with the old battle ax, I took the cuffs off.

Shortly after I took the cuffs off, the doctor reached toward the suspect's nose to examine him and then he pushed the doctor backwards. The doctor stumbled backwards, hitting the block wall. I jumped in, spun him around, and when he faced me, I let loose with a hard right punch and gave him a hard back hand on his nose that caused him to drop to his knees, crying and holding his nose. I asked the suspect "What's the matter, tough guy, it hurts?"

The doctor angrily yelled at me and demanded my name and asked me why I took the handcuffs off the suspect, and I pointed to the supervising, "War wagon nurse." I then said, "Talk to her."

I needed to get back on the streets because it was busy. The trouble is when you make an arrest, you are out of service, and the guys have to take your calls.

The female victim sustained a cracked orbital bone around her eye, and it was a very serious injury. I first booked him for battery, but when I saw the extent of the damage he inflicted on her, I went back and rebooked him for attempted murder. This new charge had higher bail, and he would stay in jail longer, giving her time to decide what to do to get away from him. Hopefully, she has some relatives that would help her out, and she needed to get her children away from the violence or they would be taken away by child protective services.

I advised her to start thinking of where to go to protect her children from the violence at least until he cooled down. She told me she would consider the options, but because she has children and did not want to displace the kids from friends and school, she would stay in the house. I told her she had the option of getting a restraining order from a judge. If the husband violates the order, he would go back to jail. I also told her there are shelters for battered women and anger management programs. I told her I would check on her from time to time before I left. The violence usually impacts the poor children who really suffer. When adults engage in this type of violence, they forget about the kids who are hiding in their rooms, shaking and crying. Children witnessing this violence firsthand can leave them emotionally scarred for the rest of their lives.

These types of calls are very dangerous for the patrol officer. Many police die in the line of duty while responding to domestic calls. Often, weapons are involved in these cases. The number 1 danger to the patrol officer is when he is expected to solve problems between two people that have been going on, sometimes for years in a couple of minutes.

Domestic Violence across the Street

One day, I was in my backyard playing with my German shepherd, and my son ran to me and grabbed my arm and started to pull me. He was telling me that the neighbor was being beat up by her husband. I told him I didn't want to get involved, and he pleaded for me to do something. Okay, I agreed to go with him to the front of the house.

The husband was beating the daylights out of his wife and had her in a headlock, then he fell on the ground on top of her and began pulling her hair and dragging her across the lawn. He began kicking her on her side and then on her head. I ran across the street and gave a hard punch in the nose. He began swinging at me, and I gave him a hard hit with the palm of my hand, which jerked his head back. Then I gave him a right upper-cut, and he went reeling backward falling on his back. He was out for five-count, and the wife pleaded for me to not hurt him anymore. I picked him up by his armpits, stood him up on his feet, and when I let loose, he fell on his face.

I used her phone and called for deputy backup and paramedics. I knew he needed medical aid because I knocked him out. The beer he was drinking had an effect on him when I hit him. I told her to tell the deputy everything, including when I hit him, and she said she didn't want to get me in trouble. I told her I wouldn't get in trouble. The deputy arrived, and I told him what I did and to take him in for spousal battery. I told him I would do the report and file a criminal complaint with the district attorney.

I hoped it would be the end of my involvement when I testified in court. No such luck, every night he would stand on his front lawn challenging me to fight him and curse me. He was usually drunk, holding a can of beer. He had a serious problem with his drinking. After five days of dealing with him, I decided to end it and went to his front door and knocked. He answered when he saw me and asked if I was going to beat him up again? I stepped back, offered my hand to shake and told him I was there to make friends with him. I told him whenever his wife gets him angry to not touch her and come over to my house and cool off. He agreed and that was the last time I had a problem with him. Yes, he did come over to my house when she made him angry. They finally split up and divorced. I had told him sometimes women can get to nagging. I really did not mean that women are all nags and told him he would make a good Taliban in the Middle East.

Beating of Helpless Female

It began on a beautiful day. It was going to be a good day for me because I received notification from the county personnel office that I was in group 1 on the list for detective. I hoped I was soon to be promoted.

I was hoping graveyard was quiet because I had a ton of paperwork to catch up on and turn in. But that is not how it went and within a few minutes I would be fighting for my life. The call began as a routine call, and it turned into a terrible situation for me. It was a family disturbance call. I walked up to the door and found the door open. I rang the doorbell, and a small boy came to the door and invited me inside. I asked him to get an adult for me. His mother walked up to the door, opening it for me to step inside. Once I got inside and followed her to the living room, she pointed to a very large Samoan man who was as big as a refrigerator. She said she wanted him out of her house and for me to get him out. I asked her who he was, and she replied, "My boyfriend." I asked him to leave, and he told me to have a sex "act" with myself. I thought to myself; this is not a good thing for me.

Here we go again. I contacted the dispatcher and requested a warrant check on him with what information the victim gave. She gave his DOB and full name as I requested. I walked in front of him and a large glass table, and the dispatcher came back to me, advising he had a felony warrant out for him for battery on a peace officer for

56

$25,000 bail. As soon as she notified me, he jumped up and gave me a hard push backward. I landed on the glass table. When I hit the table backwards, I landed on my back. It sounded like an explosion. Then he jumped on to me and started to choke me with one hand, and with his other hand, he was trying to pull my gun out of my holster. With my right hand, I placed my hand over my holster as he was trying to grab my handgun inside of my holster. With my left hand, I placed the palm of my hand against his chin, and I grabbed his hair and pulled to one side as hard as I could, but nothing was working to get him off of me.

Then suddenly, I heard someone yelling, and it was Scotty who grabbed his hair, pulling him back and then he wrapped one arm around his neck and tried to get him off me. At the same time this was going on, the female and the boy were screaming. Scotty grabbed an all-steel flashlight and hit him over the head. This was a steel flashlight called a Kel-lite that most patrol officers carry. He began to bleed on me. His blood was pouring out of his open head wound. Scotty hit him again, and finally, the man went limp on me. I rolled and slugged this guy rapidly until he fell onto me, and I pushed him off of me and told Scotty to stop hitting him before we killed him. I was concerned we may accidentally kill him, and once Scotty stopped, I gave him one forceful punch to the side of his face. He dropped. I guess between the Kel-lite and my fist both, it finally took the fight out of him. I gave him a push, and he rolled off of me.

I looked like someone who was in a car wreck. My hair was full of blood and glass. My shirt was two colors, the bottom tan and the top red. We struggled to put the handcuffs on him and bend his arms behind him. It was like trying to bend steel. I found out later he was a star rugby amateur player. Once we got him handcuffed, we stuffed him into the back of the car. He was bleeding, and I told Scotty I would take him to the hospital for his wound so we could take him to the jail for booking later. Meanwhile, I went home to change my shirt and wash the blood out of my hair and off my face. I met with Scotty and took the prisoner and proceeded to the hospital.

On the way to the hospital, he kept saying he was sorry for hurting me. He further said he liked police officers. I told him he had a strange way of showing it and now he has two charges of battery on peace officers. The problem was he does not like being in jail. He said he was sorry for pushing me on that glass table, and he was afraid of jail. I asked him what he was afraid of because he was so big no one would dare cause him trouble. He said that is not true because some guys wanted to take him on to prove how brave they are, but they would jump him while he was sitting. I asked him why he tried to get my gun—was he going to shoot me? He said he was trying to get the gun to his girlfriend so she could hide it, and so I could not shoot him. I told him, "Didn't you realize you were scaring the hell out of your girlfriend and the small boy watching all that violence?"

I told him that he has to attend an anger management class and booked him for battery on a police officer and also for the outstanding warrant. Actually, I liked him even though he was a raving nut. Maybe, just maybe, some judge would sentence the suspect to prison. I guess the judge believed fighting people is a routine part of the job. He was given three years.

I asked Scotty how he knew I was in trouble. He said he had a call last week at the same house. When he got there, the female told him that he was dangerous at that time. When he heard me run the warrant check, and it came back active, and I didn't acknowledge the dispatcher back. He came just in case it went south for me, and I needed help.

As soon as the dispatcher advised he had a felony warrant, he knew the guy was a big person. "You came just in time. He was going to get my gun and shoot me, or I would be successful in getting my gun out of my holster and shoot this nut at close-range," I told Scotty, "Thanks because I was exhausted and didn't have any energy left in me. That dope, he owes you because if I was able to get my gun, I was going to shoot once. You saved two lives in one day." I was very grateful and could not thank him enough.

He said, "You would do the same for me." Thank God he made a decision to go to the house and check on me.

Brian Shooting

One night while on patrol in a commercial business area, I was at a stoplight rubbing my sleepy eyes (the effects from working graveyard shift), when shots rang out. The sound came from the adult bookstore across the street.

I drove through the light, into the parking lot, and right up to the front door of the store. I made contact with the clerk who was standing in the open doorway. He told me two men fired a gun at him and tried to pull him over the counter because he would not give them the money. While I was at the stoplight waiting for the light to turn green, I had seen two men exit the front door and run toward a black car and drive away. I prepared to make contact with the two men. I contacted the dispatcher and advised her I was attempting to make contact with two suspects of an armed robbery with shots fired. Then I heard Deputy Brian English on the sheriff radio, and I was glad to hear the voice of my good friend. He told the dispatcher that he was going to back me.

Brian pulled in behind my sheriff's unit and began to follow me. I activated my red light and siren. The suspects refused to stop. They drove into a darkened industrial area, and we proceeded to initiate a felony car stop.

On the patrol car public address system, I ordered the driver to exit the car with his hands above his head and walk backwards toward the sound of my voice. He complied and was walking backwards toward me. I ordered him to get down on his knees. I also ordered him to place his hands on the top of his head. I saw that Brian had his weapon pointed in the suspect's direction. I slowly walked toward the kneeling suspect. When I reached him, I gripped the suspect's two hands with my left hand. I reached around my back to obtain my handcuffs to place them on him. As I reached for the cuffs, the suspect pulled out of my grip, stood up, and at the same time, spun his body around. He was now facing toward me. As he was getting up, with my right hand I removed my service revolver from its holster, at the same time Brian came to help me with this now out of control suspect. I reached out to grab his loose hand at the same time as Brian reached us. The suspect grabbed the wrist of my gun hand striking it so hard it pushed it back, pointing the gun toward Brian. Brian was reaching out to grab the suspect when the gun discharged.

I thought Brian had been shot in the stomach. Brian stepped back, grabbing his left hand with his right hand. Placing his bleeding hand into his midsection caused the blood from his hands to spread out onto the stomach area of his wool uniform jacket. Brian yelled out, "Phil, I have been shot!"

I called out a 999, which is radio code for officer down. I pulled the suspect down to the pavement onto his back. I then dropped one knee on his chest in order to stop him from struggling. I found out later that I broke his sternum. I called for an ambulance to respond for Brian. Then I heard Brian holler, "Phil, it's just my finger!"

He was in severe pain because the bullet passed through the end of his index finger where all the nerve endings are located. I was so relieved that it wasn't in the stomach as I first had thought.

Much later, I told him it helped him make it easier to pick his nose, and the bullet had caused the tip of his finger to have a hook in it. Brian didn't appreciate my warped sense of humor.

Times were much different then. No Officer Involved Shooting Team existed at that time. There was no CSI Unit to investigate the crime scene. This activity was completed by the substation officers. As a matter of fact, after Brian had been treated at the hospital, he had the deputy that was assigned to accompany him bring him back to the crime scene. Together, with Brian holding his taped up hand in the air, and under the influence of pain killers, we measured the distances and evidence markers from each other. We completed the scene investigation and ended our graveyard shift.

Today, things are much different. From headquarters, there would be a whole cadre of troops arrive at the scene, the Officer Involved Shooting Team from the homicide unit with five detectives and a sergeant, a couple of CSI investigators, a public affairs representative, and a representative from the department's psychologist's office. Everyone involved would have been placed on administrative leave and spent hours being interviewed by the team from headquarters.

When I got home that night, I was numb and couldn't sleep. I guess I was suffering from shock.. I had a sleepless night. It was difficult to go back to work the next day.

CHAPTER 2

Burglary Surveillance

One summer, we were getting hit hard with burglaries on a regular basis. All of the burglaries were placed within the area I mostly patrolled, and that was the county area of Chino. We finally traced down and discovered who the suspects were, and they were coming from the Los Serranos area.

There is a detention complex in South Chino called Boy's Republic. It is like Boys Town in the Mickey Rooney movie from the 1940s. The residents in the surrounding area knew the boys from the home were being blamed, knowing they were not guilty and were unjustly blaming these boys because some people wanted the home to be closed down.

There is a wonderful juvenile program in this Chino Hills area, and the program was fashioned after Father Flanagan's Boys Town. That movie starred Mickey Rooney and Spencer Tracy. The boys live in dormitories and had to follow the rules of the home. If they broke a rule, the boys decided the punishment. The entire program was very successful, and these abused boys were made into good young men and given a chance in life. They have a curfew and must be in their dorm by 10:00 p.m. If they are late, they are placed on a report. I always had a great and positive attitude about the facility because it was changing lives of so many boys, and they were becoming outstanding citizens later.

When there is a burglary in the area, the people are quick to blame the boys. I knew better that it was adults from the area and wanted to prove it while on graveyard shift. I did not believe the problem was the boy's home, so I went on my personal crusade to catch the real thieves.

I was cruising in a neighborhood where I knew the crook lived. It was dark, so I blacked my headlights and parked. I believed that problem was coming from the residential areas of the Glenmeade and Los Serranos areas. I spotted a car with one subject. As I was getting closer to the car, I noticed the person slide down lower in the front seat. When I saw this, I knew a crime was occurring and doubled back and watched the car when another person walked from the adjacent street with a pillow case full of something. I requested our helicopter come to my location, and once it arrived, it requested they follow the car while I drove off to another location and wanted to find out where the fence was located. A "fence" is one or more persons who take in stolen property for a dime on a dollar. They started to move, and the chopper followed the car from above, and eventually they carried the pillow case into a house. He was a known burglar going to a house he was not familiar with. I watched as the suspect walked out of the home without the pillow case. I was certain he had been carrying stolen merchandise.

I pulled up in the driveway and was now certain I found the fence. I needed another deputy to help me keep an eye on the house, so I contacted Deputy Brian English. Brian watched the house when I was off work and he was able to get some important information. I needed to write a search warrant for the house and needed license plate numbers, so I could run them on our computers for probable cause for a search warrant. I contacted informants and was told a fence lived at the property. He set up business a few months ago. Brian spotted a car that was wanted for a burglary, so he stopped him several blocks away and arrested the driver. The driver did not admit the property was stolen, but the car was. The dirt bag suspect was booked for grand theft auto. As soon as I was notified about the arrest, I wrote the search warrant and took it to a judge. Once the search warrant was signed by a judge, Brian and I were ready to rock and roll and make our move. Brian went to the house and served the warrant. We hit the house during the daylight hours and got the bastards with a house full of stolen property. The man who lived in the house was on parole from state prison. We arrested all of them, and one who was an ex-con tried to run out the back door. Brian grabbed him and pulled him into the house and handcuffed him. We found a pickup loaded with stolen property. Brian and I eventually arrested all the thieves for burglary and cleared several cases. I contacted parole officers. We had a break in the case when we rounded up the burglars in the area and found a list of phone numbers and identified people on the list. They kept good records. The burglaries stopped.

I made sure a press release was in the news about the arrest in the local papers, including an article that the sheriff believed that these were the people who were stealing property from the local neighborhoods. I wanted to hammer home that the Boys Republic was not involved. I have met almost all the boys from that facility and would give them rides to the facility so they would not violate curfew. As far as I was concerned, the boys were good boys who were dealt a lousy hand of cards between coming from broken homes and even worst abusive homes. Boys Republic is an outstanding organization that turns troubled boys into good citizens. The case Brian and I worked changed people's opinions toward the facility. Sometimes in this business, you find you are doing really worthwhile things.

Burglary Watch with Cop Mistake

Most detectives I have worked with were outstanding investigators, and I especially want to mention Johnnie Powell. John has a photographic memory for, among other things, license plate numbers. John was my partner while I was at the Fontana Station. I began working cases with him. We were finally getting caught up on the caseload when we got an in-basket stacked high. Fontana was a very busy station, and I had worked with the Sergeant Pat McCurry before while in the Narcotics Division. Pat had a top reputation in the county with enforcement communities, judges, district attorneys, and other detectives.

One day, several of us went to an area that was having problems with burglaries. This was in a low-income area, and we were looking for a particular crook. We needed some suspect information that would help reduce the problem in this neighborhood. The patrol deputies were not able help to us and had absolutely no information for us, so we decided to set up a code 5, which means surveillance in the area. We needed to blend in the area and wait for the crooks to arrive. We decided to park our car a block away. Johnnie and I stayed mobile, just in case we needed to make a car stop and the others spread out.

One detective took a position on someone's front porch, but he did a stupid thing. He waited there but had a problem and walked to the side of the house and urinated in the bushes. The homeowner called 911 and told them a crazy man was exposing himself and peeing in the bushes.

After a few hours, we had decided to call off the code 5. It was quiet, and then we were contacted by the dispatcher, requesting we handle a male, exposing himself on the same street we were on. We discovered it was one of our guys.

I asked, "What the hell is going on?"

A detective was spotted urinating in the bushes where he was hiding while we had the code 5 going on. Well, the woman who lived in the house walked to her kitchen and went to her sink and looked out the window, and that is when she discovered a man urinating on her award-winning miniature roses, and he was exposing himself. I asked where the detective was located, and we found him at the house and asked him what he was doing while he was at the house. We advised the dispatcher to cancel the call, and we would handle it and keep it low-key. The dispatcher figured out it was probably one of us. Yes, indeed, it was one of our guys.

After twenty minutes, John called me, saying he could not calm the woman down, and he needed my help. I made contact with her, and she was on the warpath. She wanted a pound of flesh and wanted him fired. We told her he was one of us, and the guy was a cop he was working very hard on a surveillance assignment. She insisted on a report being made. I told her the man was no pervert; he just made a bad choice and to give him another chance.

When I found out she was a miniature rose collector, it just happened that I had been reading an article about miniature roses and had enough information to talk "roses" with her. I offered her twice the value of the bush the cop had urinated on with an offer of one hundred dollars. She knew she was getting a great profit for the plant. I also explained to her if we were to take an official report, the detective may lose his job and could be registered as a sex offender. All he was trying to do was catch some crooks that were breaking into houses on her street, but he should have told you he was having a problem. I asked if she would accept an apology from him, and she agreed.

So we had "Detective Bozo" make contact, apologize, and the problem was solved. The woman calmed down. I collected my one hundred dollars from the detective, and he was glad to pay to keep the backlash off him so the Keystone Cop story would not become a report. She changed her mind about making the report. I told the cop he should have contacted the lady and got permission first and explained his dilemma.

John and I looked at each other with a blank look on our faces and I told John "What the hell just went on?"

We started to laugh about what we had to go through because the incident was unbelievable. It was *Keystone Cops*, *Laurel and Hardy*, and the *Three Stooges*—Larry, Moe, and Curly Joe—all rolled up in one. The kind of stuff that just went on, and you could not make it up, and it was one of the graveyard shift stories. We called off the code 5 and went back to the location without the "Bozo".

We nabbed the crooks about two weeks later and arrested them inside a house on graveyard shift. I suggested we keep this whole episode from the sergeant. I figured, what he doesn't know won't hurt him. The problem was handled. No problem, unless one of the dispatchers gives us up.

Well, then we fall on our swords. After all, John said, "We have a new rose friend."

I responded, "Okay, don't be a wise guy."

We made a car stop later in that neighborhood and got four dirt bag ex-cons who were casing the place. We arrested them all and charged them with possession of illegal narcotics.

Deputy Confronts Kidnapper

During the late afternoon, one of our deputies while off-duty went shopping with his wife to a local food store. While he was at the back of the store with his wife, a man with a loaded gun grabbed a female employee at gunpoint and dragged her out of the store with the muzzle to her head. The deputy rushed to her aid, and when he confronted the man, the suspect fired and wounded the deputy. The deputy managed to fire a few rounds, wounding the suspect. A shopper ran out of the store to assist the wounded deputy who was on the ground in serious condition and was wrestling with the suspect forcing him to the ground, letting the female go.

There is no doubt this deputy was a hero as well as the citizen for his heroic action. Both men saved the woman.

On New Year's Day, the sheriff asked me to go along with Captain Perret to Florida to attend an award ceremony for the deputy who was wounded when he tried to save women who were being held by a crazy man.

We were checking into the hotel and noticed all the widows attending the ceremony. All these women lost their husbands who were killed in action while on patrol. It was very sad to see the grieving women with their children. They were to be given awards for being the wives of these dead heroes. When we got dressed in our class A uniform for the ceremony, I wore my command uniform, a very fancy uniform, with stars with the scrambled eggs on the bill of my hat, gold buttons, and gold stripes. I looked like an army general.

The city recognized the citizen, and the country recognized the deputy at a ceremony in Florida. These officers were to receive the highest award given to an officer.

While I and Captain Ron Perret, the deputy's commanding officer, were at the ceremony, Mr. Jewell came up to me and asked to have a photograph taken with me. I agreed. During that ceremony, they announced Mr. Jewell was cleared by the FBI in that bombing at the Olympic Games in Atlanta, Georgia. Mr. Jewell was the true hero and saved many lives. Unfortunately, he was falsely accused as the bomber where several people were killed. I was very happy to meet this man who suffered greatly because he was arrested for a crime he didn't do. It was determined by the FBI that Mr. Jewell was completely innocent, and he was recognized for what he did for saving many lives by grabbing the bag containing explosives and removing it away from people.

While there, we met many women who are widows because their husbands got killed in the line of duty. All of those officers died while performing their duty on all shifts. When we were listening to each of the citations of those who died, it was obvious graveyard shift was the most dangerous.

The shift is without doubt the most dangerous of them all, and yet it must be covered by peace officers. The only way I would suggest improvement is a two-man graveyard patrol. I know two men are expensive but perhaps reserves should be scheduled on a routine basis.

Deputy Knocked Down

One graveyard shift one of the deputies made a car stop. He made contact with the driver, and when the driver stepped out of the car, he started punching the deputy, knocking him to the pavement. The suspect got advantage after the contact, and there was a struggle. He was kicking him on the head and pulled the officer's service weapon. He lowered the gun and took aim, then started to pull the trigger when a bystander ran up to the suspect and pleaded to him not to shoot the deputy. But for the grace of a good citizen, the deputy survived—thanks to that brave person. The suspect complied and left the area with the handgun. The citizen grabbed the deputy's belt radio and spoke on it, requesting help for the deputy. The citizen was a hero, and the department eventually recognized him, and he received a medal from the sheriff. This is a good example of someone who got involved and saved a life. The deputy quit the department when he realized he was seconds away from being killed. He left to look for a safer job. He has a new profession and is very happy, and so is his wife.

Several months later, another detective, Paul Kellner, and I were working late at the station and when I decided to call the suspect's girlfriend of the one who beat up the cop and took the gun. When she answered, I told her who I was. I asked her if her boyfriend made contact with her. She told me he just called her, so I asked her if she happened to hear anything that was unusual in the background. No, but she did hear the operator interrupt her on a long-distance call because the operator gave a two-minute warning to the suspect. After I talked to her, I made a quick call to the long distance operator and asked her what the location was and wanted to know when two-minute warnings are given during a long distance call.

I asked the operator, "When do you cut in and give a two-minute warning on a long distant call on a pay phone?"

She told me "Las Vegas is the only place in the country that does that."

I told Paul to call Las Vegas Metro about that kind of warning on the phone and give them the description of the suspect vehicle, including information that the suspect is armed and dangerous. A few minutes went by when Metro called back and advised us they spotted the car on Las Vegas Boulevard and got him after a short car chase. They tried to make a felony car stop, and he tried to run, but they caught him and arrested him for us. Metro also recovered the handgun.

It was very, very late that night that when the Detective Sergeant, Paul and I drove to Las Vegas to bring the suspect back to San Bernardino County. We picked him up and transported him to on one of our jails. We really lucked out getting this dirt bag in custody. We learned he had committed several bank robberies with the deputy's handgun. We booked him for battery on a police officer and for the federal warrants for bank robbery.

Officer-Assisted Suicide

For the most part, it seemed that only graveyard shift had to deal with the moon and nuts affected by the full moon. When I was a patrol officer, we had to rely on verbal skills, a night stick, and our hands. The last resort was the gun. We did not have pepper gas back in those days, but we had mace. However, I never carried it because when you use it at times the person becomes more violent.

Case in point, one call I received on a full moon night was about a family arguing. A neighbor called in about a family disturbance. I remember this call clearly. I really did something stupid and forgot officer safety precautions and placed myself in a dangerous situation.

I rolled on unknown circumstances, and when I arrived at the address, I found a woman and her children in the middle of the street. I asked her what the problem was. She said, "My husband is inside the home and he is acting crazy. He has been acting crazy most of the day and keeps punching holes in the wall with his fists and yelling at everybody threatening to kill himself. He was also drinking beer all day."

I asked her if her husband had any weapons—like a gun, knife, club, baseball bat, or anything that could hurt me.

She replied, "Nothing."

I asked her, "Are you sure?"

And she said, "Yes, absolutely. No weapons."

I asked her, "Where is he located inside the home?"

She said the last time she saw him, he was in the kitchen in the darkness. I walked to the kitchen and stepped in the doorway. The kitchen was dark, so I called his name and asked him where he was, and he replied, "Sitting at the table."

I asked him why he was sitting in the dark, and he said, "Waiting for you." As soon as he said that, I got chills up my arms.

My flashlight lit up the kitchen, and I saw him sitting there. I reached for the light switch, flipped it up and turning the lights on, and now I could see him clearly sitting at the end of the kitchen table with a blue revolver lying in front of him. He was leaning back in his chair, and his arms were folded. I told this nut not to do anything stupid, not to move his hands toward the gun, and I pulled my Glock 9 mm out of my holster and pointed at him, telling him not to make a move and do what I tell him to do. I thought about incidents that were called officer-assisted suicides. I certainly did not want to shoot him. I did not want to be placed in a position like that, and it always ends up messy for the officer.

He said, "The gun is not for you—it is for me, I am going to kill myself." I ordered him to stand up and step away from the table. He complied, and I took a deep breath of relief. I should have used another method of getting him to comply rather than using my gun. I told him if he went for the gun, I would put six into him before he got one off. When he stood up, I told him to walk toward me. As soon as he reached me, I put the handcuffs on, and I told him he was not arrested; but I placed the handcuffs on him for his safety and mine, and I was going to take him to a place where he will get some help.

After I took him out of the house, I told his wife that it would be a good idea to place the gun on the kitchen table somewhere safe where the kids wouldn't be able to get hold of it. She asked, "What gun?" as if she knew nothing about it.

I placed a 5150 hold on him. This meant a psychological evaluation would be done on him, and they could give him some pills to help out with his depression.

As I was taking the suspect to the county mental ward to place a seventy-two-hour hold on him for observation, I told him he needs a few pills and that he will feel better. He responded by telling me to drop dead, so he received no other advice from me. He told me he was going to kill himself as soon as he was released. I asked him, "What about your wife and children, your family will suffer without you."

He said, "I am going to lose my job soon."

I told him, "That was no reason."

He told me he didn't want to talk about it and to mind my own business. I told him that if he must kill himself, then do it on day shift when his kids are in school.

I told him, "I was certainly not an expert, but it sounds like you are suffering from depression." I suggested he get some antidepressants from a doctor. He told me to mind my own business again. I told the staff at the ward what he told me.

I was really angry at the woman outside for not mentioning a gun. Oh well, I can't blame her. I was really careless. Guess I was tired, and normally, I am very cautious and don't get into this type of situation. That night, I learned a lesson that there is no time to be tired. I must be alert because my life depends on it at all times.

Toy Gun Robbery

One night during the busy time of the year, close to Christmas and considered robbery season, my shift ended. And the sergeant watch commander told John and I to go home and not to get involved in anything. We were very busy with cases, we had that week and up to our eyeballs in work. I was driving John Powell home, and we stumbled upon an armed robbery in progress that turned into a car chase, shooting, and capture of a robber with a toy gun.

We came upon an auspicious suspect who was waiting in a car parked right next to a 7-Eleven store with his car idling. He was wearing a black knit cap and was slumped on his seat, trying to conceal himself. All earmarks of an armed robbery to be committed. We made a U-turn, then drove up the street with our headlights off and parked across the street. We had a good view of the store. Sure enough, he walked inside the building, holding a gun, and pointed it at the store clerk. She raised her arms over her head, and we knew he was robbing the store. After he grabbed the money and ran to his car, he drove away at a high rate of speed. We were right behind his car and activated our red lights and siren that made him drive faster and more recklessly blowing Stop signs and speeding going dangerously fast. The dispatcher advised other patrol cars to head our way. I heard the dispatcher over the police radio, advising of our location. She gave our most recent location to the units. The radio got busy, and it was going nonstop. We could hear the sirens of the other sheriff units approaching. When we attempted to arrest the suspect, he led us on a high-speed chase. The suspect eventually stopped and pulled onto dirt in a section of the main road right next to an orange grove. He slid the car, bailed out of his car, still carrying the gun, and began to run toward a residential area. We stopped behind him, and I jumped up with one foot still in the car and yelled for him to freeze. He turned toward me with the gun still in his hand, and I ordered him to drop the gun; he refused. In order to safeguard innocent people living in this residential area, I had to shoot at him so he would stop and give himself up. Then I fired six rounds at him but missed him. Though he fell to the ground. We thought I shot him. I caught up with him and slapped the handcuffs on.

Normally, I am accurate when I shoot my gun. At the range, I qualified shooting every month. I will admit I was not consistent in getting the bullet on the bull's-eye. Sometimes I can't miss, and it dazzled the mind. I usually do all right but jumping out of a car coupled with my target running in a zigzag fashion instead of a straight line was not easy. This graveyard night I was very happy that I missed my target. I have been lucky so far that I had not had to shoot and kill someone in the line of duty.

Because the suspect was using a toy gun that resembled a steel gun, committed an armed robbery, and refused to stop for a police officer; and I was justified in shooting the suspect, the press would have a field day The clerk did not know it was a toy gun, nor did I. We believed it was the real McCoy. I would have felt badly if I had killed him, and the press would have gone crazy.

I could imagine the headlines the next morning: "Wild out-of-control and trigger-happy deputy shoots and kills an unarmed man holding a simple plastic toy. The same gun a six-year-old uses when playing cops and robbers."

God was good to me that day, and I was lucky that I was a lousy shot that night. I would not have been forgiven and would have to go through a lot of crap from the department. I would be described as that maniac killer in a cop's uniform, and the public would want a complete investigation and call in demanding the deputy be fired and for the sheriffs resignation.

The problem is we had to make major life or death decisions, and it takes time to learn how to handle those situations.

The gods were good to me, and I was lucky that day, but so was the suspect—lucky that I was a lousy shot that night. His gun was a look-alike toy gun. He said one bullet passed through his hair. I told him he was a lucky man "It was not his time to die tonight." It was a good thing I was not using my automatic Glock gun. The six-shot revolver was not very accurate. Now I know what you are thinking. Okay, I admit. I was a lousy shot that night.

He went to prison for the robbery. This clown's luck ran out. He was released from prison, and a few months later, he was found in the street—dead—a few blocks from his house, lying in a dirt road with two bullets in the back of his head. The shooting looked like an execution by someone that was a better shooter than I was. It was probably during a dope burn. He had no toys, just burglary tools. The police never found the killer. I believe they put very little effort out on the case because he was an example of human garbage.

Capture of a Robbery Suspect

I heard the dispatcher over the police radio, advising other units to assist us while she announced our location. The traffic got very busy and was going nonstop with others, acknowledging that they were responding to the emergency broadcast. We could hear the sirens as the patrol units were approaching.

The suspect pulled onto a dirt section of the road off the main street and adjacent to the orange grove. When the door opened, the suspect jumped out and started to run, still carrying the gun in his right hand as he ran toward the residential area. John skidded to a stop as I jumped and yelled at the suspect to stop or I will shoot; he ignored me and kept on running. I fired two shots, and the suspect dropped down to the ground. John thought I hit him, and I thought I did also. When I ran up to the suspect, I looked at his face, and I noticed he was blinking. I asked him if he was shot.

He replied, "You missed me. I think one of the bullets went through my hair." Was glad I missed him because a short time later, I found out he used a toy gun that looks like the real thing. I had reasonable and probable cause to shoot at him, trying to stop him before he entered the residential area. He was very lucky I missed him and fortunate that I did not kill him. My bullets missed him.

I guess he ran out of luck when someone didn't miss him. He was found later by a man walking his dog and was shot to death during a dope deal that went south for him. This time, someone used a real gun.

Gay Kidnap and Robbery

One morning, I was given a report by the detective sergeant. It was a case involving a kidnap. According to the report, a gay man and his gay friend were kidnapped while at a rest stop. Two men wearing ski masks over their heads and armed with a gun placed the gay men in a van and drove them to a remote location. Both men were robbed and forced to take off all their clothing while the two suspects kept threatening both men that they would be killed when the van stopped. They were kicked out of the van, and the suspects left them on the side of the road naked. As cars were approaching, they were forced to jump into the bushes to hide. They finally reached a phone booth and called a friend who responded and picked them up. They further told me many of their gay friends did not report the kidnappings and robberies to the police. They were kidnapped the same way. I asked how many of their friends were assaulted by these men, and whether it occurred late in the night. The men told me the reason they all hang out at the rest stop is because they are able to meet other gay men and felt embarrassed about being gay.

I rounded up all these gay men and had they came in the station. I began to interview all of them, and when I finished with gathering the information I needed, I told the sergeant that I wanted to set up a stakeout at the rest stop and have one of the undercover narcotic detectives play the role as a gay guy and park an unmarked car at the location, and when the detective invites them to get in the car, we would surround the vehicle and take the kidnappers into custody. We wanted to set up surveillance and catch them in the act.

One night, we had an IS-wheeler and an unmarked car. We waited until the suspects arrived. Eventually, the suspects drove up. The car we had planted was alongside the truck, and we were watching the car drive up behind our car with the detective inside by himself. They approached the car. He lifted his hand and raised it to give the arrest signal. He waved the "don't move" signal with his hand. Then moved in and got the guys. We took three men into custody. We booked them for kidnapping. When they appeared in court, they pled guilty to kidnapping, and they got fifty years each. The judge was hard on them.

The suspects lived in West Covina, so I did a search warrant to their apartment address. We went to arrest another suspect who was the brains behind the crimes. These very dopey kidnappers were sentenced to state prison for fifty years. We found the wallets of many of the victims and located the gun. Eventually, Cal Trans closed the rest stop because there were too many complaints about men having sex in the bathrooms. The suspects were not real hardcore criminals.

Armed Robbery

One day during graveyard shift, on my day off, I pulled up to a liquor store for a soda. When I walked up to the door of the store and looked through the glass door, I noticed the customers were on their knees, and their hands were above their heads. I whispered to a man near the door, "Is the robber still in the store?"

He whispered back to me, "Yes, he is behind the counter."

I asked "How many?"

And he replied, "Just one."

I backed away from the door and waited for the robber to walk out of the store. I did not want to go into the store and feared someone could get hurt if I got into a gun fight. I asked for backup, requesting another deputy and advised dispatch to send assistance with no sirens. I did not want to alert the robber. He finally came out and started running. As soon as he stepped out, I nabbed him and put him under arrest at gun point. He was taken to the jail and booked for armed robbery.

This is an example of why we all carry our guns off-duty. There are some states that do not allow this. New York, for example. Also, guns are banned on commercial air flights. I believe there should be a federal law that allows off-duty guns in this country.

The Concert

One morning, the captain called me into his office and told me he had an investigation that he wanted me to handle. It was a robbery from the Us Concert at Glen Helen Park. It was a very large concert, and one of the biggest ever held in San Bernardino County. Some say this concert was larger than Woodstock. The main entertainer was Willy Nelson. There were supposed to be sixty thousand attending, and I thought this was going to be one tough case. I am going to have to figure out from sixty thousand people who committed the grand theft. This concert brought in close to one hundred thousand people, all well-behaved and having a good time. Deputies were hired to work security for the event.

I zeroed in on the victim who was an employee for a T-shirt vendor. The vendor reported one of his employees was kidnapped last night on the graveyard shift as he was taking proceeds from the sale of shirts. The employee was going to take all the money home for safekeeping, and next, he would deposit the money when the bank opened for business.

I was telling a good friend about the case where the victim claims he was kidnapped by one lone gunman who knocked him out while he was driving. The robber gave him instructions to drive nearby and go behind a supermarket. He followed the suspect's instructions, then the robber struck him over the top of his head with his handgun. The victim said he passed out, and when he regained consciousness, the robber was gone and so was the money—all fifty thousand dollars. He was able to describe the suspect as Mexican with black hair and brown eyes.

A close friend of mine, Bud Canady, suggested I make contact with the County Coroner and tell him the story that the victim gave about being knocked out and see what the doctor says. A few days later, I went to the coroner and described to him how the victim was knocked out sitting in the car. The doctor told me exactly what I thought he would say that the victim was lying and was full of BS. There is not enough space from the victim's top of his head and the roof interior (six inches) to the head, and the suspect could not have enough leverage to build up the force he would need to knock him out. The doctor gave me good enough information to put in place a search warrant. I never thanked Bud and had been busy, plus I forgot when I was looking for the victim who was gone with the wind.

I was told the victim moved to Las Vegas with no forwarding address. However, I knew where his wife's mother was living in Las Vegas. I hoped that I would be able recover the entire amount, which was fifty thousand dollars from the sale of the event T-shirts. I discussed the case with Sergeant McCurry and advised him I would have to take a trip to Las Vegas. The employee lived with his wife at an unknown address. I planned to watch the wife at her mother's home because she was eight months pregnant, and I had a hunch she visited her mother frequently and would stay close to mom in the event something happened because of her condition. If everything goes right, when she is on the move, I would follow her right to our boy. I took another deputy with me to help follow her. It is always better when two sets of eyes are watching.

We left for Las Vegas and arrived early in the morning. My hunch was paying off. Her car was at her mother's house. We waited for about an hour until she got in her car and began to drive. I was driving, and we did not realize how busy the strip was with heavy traffic. To stay with her was a nightmare. We had to blow a couple of red lights while avoiding crashing into taxi cabs in order to keep up with her. The traffic was bumper-to-bumper in the intersections, so we had to maneuver to get through. I had said five Hail Mary prayers to myself.

She decided to go gambling, so she drives in to the MGM casino area. We followed her into the casino's parking lot, then she walked into the casino, and we almost lost her. The casino was packed with gamblers, but lucky for us, she was the only person who was really big and pregnant. She sat down in front of a slot machine and played for about ten minutes until she played long enough for the one-armed bandit to take her money. She got up and was on the move again. Next, she goes to an ATM and does more gambling; and this time, she hits a small jackpot. She left the casino and got in her car and drove off.

It was important she continue to her husband, so we could locate him. She left the main boulevard and drove into an apartment complex and parked her car, then she was on the move—on foot. We watched her walk to an apartment and knock, and when the door opened, I could see our suspect standing by the door, talking to his wife. And then she walked into the apartment. Well, what do you know, it is our suspect who lets her in now; and I began to write the warrant.

I needed time to get to a judge that was still in court. I telephoned Metro to meet me nearby the complex so I could hitch a ride to the station and the courthouse about thirty minutes away to do the search warrant. When they arrived, I asked them to take me to the station while the other deputy continued to watch the apartment, in case the suspect left. When I got to their station, I typed the entire warrant for presentation to the judge. One of the sergeants took me to the judge. I was taken to one of the judges, and I handed him the search warrant. I explained what we were doing here in their city, and he signed it and approved the warrant for nighttime or daylight hours. He read it and signed it without any questions except he told me, "Welcome to Sin City."

I decided to serve the warrant at night. The Metro officer drove me back to my car and the deputy still at the apartments, and I asked for some Metro officers to stay with us until we served the warrant. It had just become dark when we approached the door.

I announced, "Police and I have a search warrant, open the door."

There was a short delay. I entered first and yelled out, "Everyone, place their hands above their heads."

The deputy, three Metro officers, and I hit the apartment. I had kicked the door open with such force door came off its hinges.

We got her husband as he was cutting the cocaine, using baby formula trying to increase the size so he could double his money. The pile of cocaine was worth fifty thousand dollars. There was about two pounds of coke, and that is where the fifty thousand dollars went from the theft. The wife was shaking by the doorway and began to scream. I told the deputy to calm her down and that I did not want her to give birth while we were there.

Metro was happy because they received a large amount of drugs. I did not get any money back for the T-shirt vendor. All that cocaine and no money left to return to the victim. I told the suspect he really screwed up because your wife is going to have your baby in jail now. Metro took possession of the dope after we took pictures of the stash and of the suspect with the police. I left a search warrant with Metro and returned the search warrant to the judge before we left and went home.

I did not want to spend the night in Las Vegas, so we left the wife with Metro. I was grateful they took her because she was really pregnant. We took the husband with us back to San Bernardino and booked him in our jail. I interviewed him when we got to the station, and he told us he needed money because his wife was pregnant. So he figured his plan was to claim he was robbed by a crook who took the money. When he got to Las Vegas, he bought the cocaine and figured he could double his money. The suspect told me he was not a real bad guy and never broke the law. I told him, "You mean you thought you could have gotten away with it without getting caught."

Subsequently, several months later, the suspect pled guilty to stealing the money to pay for the cocaine he was going to sell in Las Vegas. He would face grand theft charges in California. He received a five-year sentence to state prison. After he does his time for the theft of the money, he must stand trial in Nevada for possession of cocaine. His wife was given probation and allowed to have her baby out of jail. Later, I heard they divorced.

CHAPTER 3

Vigilante Justice

One day on graveyard shift, a call came in to respond to a residence with an unknown problem. When I arrived, there was a dead body in the backyard. When I entered into the backyard, there was a male adult lying dead by the back sliding glass door that was leading to the kitchen. The strange thing was he had a screwdriver in his hand, and there were tool marks notched on the door, and the residents were not home. This dead guy was trying to get into the house. He was known to me as a big thief who lived in the area. Someone using a high-powered rifle with a good scope shot this guy—because this crook was shot in the back from a long distance by a sharp shooter. This is a clear example of vigilante justice doing some work for us. The killer was never found.

Gangs

We received a call that motorcycle gang members were grabbing the nozzle away from people and cutting in front of them at gas stations in Amboy. The victims were threatened with harm if they didn't cooperate. We positioned ourselves and watched the gas pumps at the crime location. We dressed in plain clothing, and there was no incident so the men drove into Laughlin for intelligence information. Nothing occurred while we were watching, so we left the area.

Johnnie and I stopped an outlaw gang motorcycle member in Fontana. It was late and dark. His name was Three Finger Perry, and we had received some information that he was carrying some meth, and he had an attitude problem, so I asked if he was carrying some dope.

He said, "No and f---k you."

I told him, "We are going to have to search you because we don't believe you."

So I had him drop his pants so that he was standing in his underwear when there was no traffic on the road, and no one saw him, but it still drove him crazy while we were at the curbside on the street. There was no dope, so I told this punk to get his pants up. The criminal had nothing coming to him because he was a member of the Vegas. We let him go.

About an hour later, we stopped a car and got the driver out of the car. He was very drunk, and we had a patrol deputy meet us at our location. We were supposed to be going home, however, we got busy. When we finally headed home, it was late, and we ended our shift.

Shootout

At the beginning of swing shift and to graveyard shift, the narcotics division was notified there was a major shootout in Riverside. The department was notified by Riverside sheriff that they were in pursuit of bank robbers, and they had a shootout with the bandits. Riverside advised us that when their officers arrived at the bank robbery scene, they were met with heavy gunfire with automatic weapons and other high powered weapons. We were told the suspects were also throwing explosives from their vehicle, a new pickup truck. Two of the suspects were in the back bed of the truck. The suspects had killed one of their officers, and they were heading our way, so we jumped in our units and joined in on the pursuit.

The department has a large air force of helicopters because it is the largest county in the nation of mostly desert and mountains. Four of our helicopters were above the suspects. The suspects began throwing homemade bombs at the pursuing patrol car. They also began shooting at the aircraft, hitting one of the four helicopters flying above the bank robbers. Some of the bullets hit the battery of one of the choppers causing it to break off from the pursuit on land. The helicopter was forced to make an emergency landing and was heading toward Lytle Creek at the back of Mount Baldy, a mountain range in San Bernardino County.

When we finally reached the area of the pursuit, the suspects were in the mountain area behind Mount Baldy. It was dark, and they spread the narcotics division to areas on the side of the mountain. We were told to wait in one location, just in case they came our way. Later I was told our deputies were right behind them as they were driving up the mountainside. They made a sharp turn at the curve and jumped out of the truck and waited for the deputy to reach them so they could ambush him as he was coming around. They opened fire on the deputy. His car was fired on with many bullets, ripping through the tin metal bullets whizzing past him. The deputy had to crawl out of his patrol car. As we were racing forward to try to catch up with the rest of the patrol cars, Deputy Dan McCarty got behind the suspects then drove around the comer. All of them jumped out of their car with machine guns waiting for him to come around the turn as soon as he did they opened up with automatics. Dan's car was a hail of bullets, and Dan skidded to a stop. Bullets were flying all around him. Dan was able to open the passenger door and get to the back of the bullet-ridden car, and finally he was able to pull his gun and fire back. Dan found himself in heavy gun battle at the same moment he was trying to stay alive while the bandit tried to kill him. This brave officer engaged into fierce gun battle. Even though he was outgunned, he stood his ground. Firing and reloading several times. The air was full of bullets, all of them heading toward him. Dan crawled toward the back of his car for better cover and had to expose himself to the gunfire when he opened up with a blaze of bullets of his own, striking one of them and the cowards started running for their lives.

We later learned that just prior to this shootout, there was an Ontario officer in front of Dan by several hundred yards. Dan looked to the side of the road and realized that an Ontario patrol unit was shot, and an officer was seriously injured. He ran to the stricken officer and tried to stop the blood gushing from his head. He was placed in a dangerous position, trying to help the officer, but he was already dead. They killed him. We knew Dan was in a big gunfight, and we all held our breath, hoping he would survive because the gun battle was fierce. We all could hear guns blasting away ahead of us. Someone counted the bullet holes in Dan's car, and they found five hundred-plus bullet holes. It was a miracle Dan survived that gun battle. He fought this gun battle with just handguns against their machine guns.

Dan eventually received and deserved the highest medal and officer could receive for bravery The Frank Bland Medal of Honor. We were all happy for Dan.

We spent the entire graveyard shift, looking for the rest of the suspects. LAPD came out to assist us with their SWAT. They found them hiding under bushes and made the big mistake of turning toward the team with guns in hand. They were killed during other shootouts with law enforcement. The money was recovered, and we found several homemade bombs and over one thousand rounds of ammunition in the truck. All I can say to the suspects is "Adios, bozos."

Days later, we discovered these bandits were planning this robbery for many months and had their getaway plans, including making bombs. After this incident, the sheriff purchased mini 14s for all the units. We all appreciated it. Once we got the weapons, we began to train with them at the range. They were semi-automatics, and SWAT got the fully automatics.

Before this, we carried lever-action—in other words, cowboy guns. The sheriff was a cowboy, and his executive staff were real cowboys; and they all owned horses—at least they thought they were. They turned in their spurs and replaced cowboy boots for wing-tip shoes. Some of these fellows were hardcore cowboys, they refused to modernize at first, but then gave in. Except the real cowboy, Sheriff Tidwell. He still was involved in rodeos, and so was his son Danny Tidwell. He was a great sheriff, and when he retired, his Undersheriff Williams took over and modernized the department. Both men made the sheriff's department one of the most respected in the country.

Bar Fights

Well, the fun was over when a big fight started in the local area, and we cleared for a code 3. That means red lights and sirens. When we got there, we spotted a man with a baseball bat. I told Brian I will take the guy with the bat you take the other five guys. I took the bat from the suspect at gunpoint, then went to Brian to help him with the five morons up against the wall. The suspects were up against the wall doing the leg spread with their hands on the wall. The fight was in a parking lot in front of the bar. We did not arrest anyone because they all complied with us. The night ended up with very busy neighbors fighting and arguing all night. It was another "crazy full moon night."

The next night at the station before graveyard began, a dispatcher poked her head in the briefing room. She advised us that we need you guys to go 10-8 from briefing because there was a big fight at one of the local bars involving twenty or more people. A 10-8 means "respond by getting in your patrol cars and going."

When we arrived at the location, there was a large group of men fighting. I jumped out of my car and grabbed two of the drunken men who were engaged in a fist fight. One of them took a swing at me but missed. I spun him around and threw a punch, and he landed against a telephone pole. He went down, and I placed the handcuffs on him. Every deputy was in combat with these dopes. We took away various weapons, bottles, buck knives, and two handguns.

It took three ambulances to take the injured to the hospital, and the rest went to jail. The fight was over a girl. None of the deputies were injured.

All night, we broke up fights, and we loaded up the jail cells that night. We looked like train wrecks. Almost all of us had blood on our uniforms. After the fight was over, we arrested several suspects and booked them with following charges: Possession of the drugs methamphetamine, cocaine, and marijuana; illegal weapons; battery on a peace officer; and drunk in public. Almost all of them were illegal aliens who were Hispanic. We put them on an immigration hold after booking them and notified the border patrol to send officers to the jail to pick them up.

Easter Party on the Dairy Farms

We received a call to break up a large party. Several units were assigned to this. I arrived first at the location, and there were a couple of hundred kids from the dairy farms located in this area. These kids were blowing off steam and said they were on Easter vacation.

I had a reserve with me as a rider, and as soon as we arrived, there was at least one hundred bottles thrown at us. I notified the dispatcher that I needed assistance. I backed the patrol car way out and put a distance between those bottles and me.

I could hear the Rancho deputies from the brand-new City of Rancho Cucamonga. I knew all of them, and they were outstanding troops and seasoned professionals. As soon as they arrived at the scene, we broke up the party, and we took a few of them to jail. They were booked for being drunk and disorderly.

Big Game Hunter

As a patrol officer on graveyard, I often felt like a big game hunter searching for criminals. These are the same criminals who break into your home during Christmas and steal all the gifts under the tree while you and your family are away. It was too bad we weren't allowed to mount their heads on the walls of the station like big game hunters do with tigers, lions, etc.

During my patrol days, I met many nice folks, and I also had to deal with the usual dopes. Some of these dopes were really mean, violent people. While you are sleeping in the safety of your home, some of these people just never sleep. They spend their nights only causing trouble. When we run up against these folks, it very seldom has a happy ending. After downing a few beers, some of the dopey guys think they are supermen, ready to take on anyone. Instead, they usually wind up in the hospital.

Girl Stabbed

It was the beginning of my shift, and I arrived at my beat. Soon after I arrived and pulled off the street and was rolling into the parking lot of a large supermarket in Chino, I happened to be looking ahead and spotted a man walking behind a young girl who was about twelve or thirteen years old. Suddenly the man pulled out a large knife and pushed the girl to the pavement. He raised the knife and plunged it into the girl's back. I maneuvered my car around and through people walking and cars desperately trying to get to this poor child. Before he stabbed her again, I watched him standing over her, and as he raised the knife over his head, I jumped out of the car. I wanted to take a shot at him, but there were too many people and cars, and I feared an innocent bystander would get hurt. So I turned on the siren and red lights. When the suspect heard the siren, he looked up, and I yelled, "Stop, put down the knife."

The suspect started running. I decided to get to the victim and help her, and using my handheld radio, I requested paramedics to the scene.

I ran up to the child, and she was having difficulty breathing. The blood over her wound was bubbling, and I knew it was a sucking wound. That knife had penetrated her lung, and as I kept my hand over her wound, I asked a person nearby to help by getting into my trunk. I threw the keys and told him to get the blanket in the trunk and bring it to me. I was lucky there was another patrol unit nearby, and I gave the description of the suspect. I knew the girl was going into shock. I wanted to keep her warm, and the other deputy, Steve Moran, advised he had caught the suspect and brought him to me and told me the location where he was apprehended. When I asked the suspect his name, I knew immediately he was mentally ill.

The child was transported to the local hospital and she survived. Her parents were very grateful to me for saving their daughter. I told them I was in the field at the right time and at the right location. I told the father the suspect was insane and that the suspect said he stabbed the victim because the voices told him to. The father wanted to tell the sheriff how happy he was with the department. I told him we are just doing our jobs.

Stabbing Victim

One evening, I was the duty detective at the Fontana Station and was called to go to Kaiser Hospital in Fontana because there was an adult male there who was the victim of a stabbing. I drove to the hospital and entered the emergency room. When I arrived and made contact, I found the victim sitting on a bench with a big twelve-inch butcher knife through his upper left thigh. I asked him how he got the knife in his leg. He told me he didn't remember and did not want to tell me anything.

His ear was partially missing with the missing part of the ear in the shape of a bite wound. Someone took a bite out of his ear, and this dope couldn't remember what happened. I questioned him about who caused the stabbing. He finally told me it happened while he was attending a barbeque.

It got more bizarre as I was questioning him, so I left the hospital and went to the crime scene—which was at the backyard of a home. There were ten deputies detaining twenty-nine people in the backyard where the group was having a barbeque. The deputies believed one person in this group was the suspect who did the stabbing. I told the deputies to take all these drunks to the station so I can interview them all and find out who did what. They all left for the station, and one deputy stayed behind with me, and before we left we both watched a large black pussy cat jump on the Weber type

grill and take a crap on the chicken. There was also dope parapher-
nalia all over the ground.

I arrived at the station, and it was very noisy because of the
drunks from the barbeque. I told the deputies to throw these loud
mouth drunks in a jail cell so we can get some order in the station
until I get to them. Tell them they are not under arrest yet. I intended
to find out the ones that were under the influence. I did not leave the
house for nothing and intended to put somebody in jail. I checked
each one and found five that were under the influence of heroin.

After questioning all twenty-nine of the suspects, the last one
talked after I told him twenty-eight people told me he stabbed the
victim and tried to kill him, so I booked him for attempted murder.
I told him the victim died from the knife wound because his main
artery was cut, and he was on life support systems. After I told him
all this baloney, he told me who did it. I taped his statement. I went
to the jail cell where my suspect was, and I took him to my office and
gave this jerk his rights. After five minutes, he admitted to the stabbing. He claimed it was self-defense. I asked him to explain, and he
told me the victim threw a red hot charcoal at him and hit his head,
so he grabbed a knife and stabbed the victim while he was sitting.
He told the victim he was going to stab him in the neck if he threw
another piece of charcoal. I asked him, "When did you bite his ear
off?" That is when he laughed at me and told me they were standing
by the barbeque after he took a bite from his ear and he spit it on the
grill in front of him. I booked this moron for mayhem and assault
with a deadly weapon. When I took this case to the DA, he told me,
"You have got to be kidding me! Do you think the talking witness is
going to testify? The filing DA told me it looks like mutual combat.
The case never went to court. I had told the deputies to throw them
into a cell until I was ready to talk to them one by one. When I got
to the owner and finished my investigation, the owner invited me to
his home to have some chicken. I told him I was allergic to cats. The

chicken has a secret sauce, and I was thinking while I was driving that when they get back to the house and eat that chicken they will enjoy the new taste thanks to the kitty cat. I finished with this bozo and let him go home to eat his wonderful chicken.

We did nothing about the stabbing because the victim did not want to cooperate. As far as I was concerned, no victim, no crime.

CHAPTER 4

Entire Family Murdered

It was early in the morning when the telephone ringing ended my restful sleep. I worked late last night because of a late investigation.

I got dressed in a suit I recently purchased—a nice Italian-cut style that was dark blue. So now I was on my way, and it was about a twenty-minute drive to the scene. I arrived at Old English Road located in a beautiful area that was known as Chino Hills. There are very expensive homes and almost all the homes had well-groomed corrals with many different kinds of horses. All of the horses were thoroughbred including Arabians. I knew what those horses looked like from the others because I was in love with the actress Kim Novak, and I knew she raised Arabians. I guess I was a typical teenager who had a schoolboy's crush on a movie star.

At the crime scene for the first time...

When I reached the driveway of the home, Detective Billy Arthur of the Homicide Division was there. He was a very well-respected detective. I refer to Billy in past tense because the department lost Billy a few years back. He was a wonderful guy, and all of us lost a good friend when he passed away.

Billy told me there are bodies all around the master bedroom. He described the victims as a male adult on the floor, leaning against the bed with his head split wide open. One of the male's fingers was lying on the carpeted floor. There was an adult female on the center of the floor with numerous stab wounds to her chest area. Two children were dead, and one young boy had been transported to the hospital.

I asked Billy what he wanted me to do for him. At that time, I was assigned to this mass killing case. He asked me to get hold of my informants and see if you can find any information. I left the scene and drove to a nearby prison called CIM for men. I wanted to find out if by chance there were any escapes recently. They advised me that they had one escape late last night. I requested all the information they had on him. The watch commander handed me a folder, and upon looking at it, I found a photograph of a black male. He was classified as violent.

Prison personnel's major blunder. The commander admitted they screwed up. They allowed him to get outside to exercise into the minimum security yard, and he jumped the chain link fence and got away. His name was listed as Creeper. I rushed the information to Billy before the brass arrived and could get in the way of the investigation.

When I arrived back at the crime scene and gave Billy the prison file of the escapee. I found Billy at the back of the home, writing his notes. He was standing by the sliding glass door, leading into the master bedroom. When I walked up to Billy, I looked through the glass doors and was stunned that the bedroom was full of bodies. I looked through the glass door from outside not wanting to enter the home and contaminate the crime scene by my footprints. I am supposed to be hardened—after all, I am a cop, but that scene shocked me.

How could a person slaughter human beings. I thought that when the children heard the two adults screaming, they ran to the master bedroom. As the killer was stabbing and hitting the adults with another weapon, possibly an ax, the children then became victims also. I believed it may be an ax because the man's head was split open with brain matter exposed.

I told Billy the children ran to the adults to seek protection, and when the poor children ran into the master bedroom, they only ran into a killing machine. I said to myself as I looked up. "Please, God. Please help us find the killer before the murders someone else."

Then Billy turned to me and said, "God, please bless these poor souls."

There were different colors of scenery present that day. The sky was a beautiful deep blue with bright clouds with silver linings, but the crime scene was colored blood red in the room where death resided. I left with a sense of co-determination. My search began for informants. My network of about fifty people was developed through the many years I was on patrol. I had built a small army of them. After making contact with all of them before my shift was over, I told them a major murder in the area with children involved had happened. I knew they would get busy checking around and let me know of anything of importance. Maybe I would be lucky.

Well, the hunt began for Creeper and the department's Sheriffs Identification Division spent several days at the scene. There was tremendous pressure on the department to get the killer of the family.

Murder suspect identified, and the department was positive they got the killer. After Creeper was apprehended by law enforcement up north, the department notified the media of his arrest. As soon as it came out in the press, the public calmed down. This was a good example of different law enforcement agencies working together for the greater good.

Creeper eventually appeared in San Diego Superior Court where he was found guilty of murder. After the verdict, he was transferred to maximum security prison in this state.

I thought to myself, *Creeper is still alive, and five people are dead by that maniac—thanks to liberal California.*

Some bleeding heart liberal believed he was innocent and should be released. This person was going to contact a very famous movie star to convince him to use his influence to have the governor give Creeper a pardon. After Creeper was in prison, I received word that a very famous Oscar-winning actor, who will stay unnamed, was convinced that Creeper was not guilty, and San Bernardino Sheriff Department set him up to take the blame because he was black. Creeper claimed he was innocent, even though we had a mountain of evidence against him. I was surprised a famous superstar and Academy Award winner was concerned that Creeper was innocent. When I heard on the radio, the crazy announcement that an actor was going to the governor, I made a beeline home and wrote an e-mail to the governor requesting that before he makes a bad decision., to please contact the department and talk with us and not endanger the public. He must have his sentence carried out. I also suggested the governor take a trip to San Bernardino and contact the sheriff's office and take a look at crime photographs, and he would quickly realize who killed these people.

This person is a savage, not only killing a family but slaughtering people. When he completed the murders, he went to the kitchen and made himself something to eat, and then took the family car and drove to San Diego—and then he went to Mexico. We put out a broadcast for the car that was already in Mexico. Apparently, he talked to and befriended a couple from northern California who had a boat, and he offered to work as a deck hand for free if they gave him a ride to Northern California, and they agreed and took him in. He was safe from apprehension for a while. The couple was lucky they were not killed by him and their boat stolen while Creeper sailed into the sunset.

Murder suspect was captured in Northern California. The local police captured him with the couple. While we were going crazy looking for him, he was enjoying a cruise up the coast. We checked out over two hundred sightings from all over the country. I was at the command post manning the telephones, and we had people calling from all over the country. One person claimed Creeper was at a baseball game sitting in the VIP box. There were many sighting calls that were no help and a wild goose chase.

He was very busy, escaping from prison and taking a trip to Mexico. Oh, by the way, he also murdered a family—both adults and all the children—and tried to kill the little boy next door. He thought he killed the boy by slitting his throat. This scumbag did not know the boy was playing dead, and it saved his life. Yes, Mr. Creeper was busy that week. Of course, he deserved a relaxing trip by yacht up the coast. Why not, he worked very hard. I hope there is a little corner in hell waiting for him.

I do not fault this actor as he was going by and believing the information he was given by someone who was very convincing. I don't know if my e-mail convinced the governor not to listen to the actor. That actor never made contact with the governor, and Creeper was never released and still remains in prison.

Gruesome Body

I went to the county gas station and filled up the gas tank in the patrol unit. As I was leaving, a call came in of suspicious circumstances, so I proceeded to the address. When I arrived, I pulled on to the driveway when a man approached me and told me a bad smell was coming from his next-door neighbor. He was worried about this neighbor.

I went to the front door and knocked, but there was no response. The smell almost knocked me over. I tried the door handle, and the door swung open, and there were flies all over the place. The odor was very strong, and it was choking me. I yelled her name, and two dogs came to the front door, and they were happy to see me. I stepped in the living room, and that is when I saw the body. It was bloated up, and I could see what was keeping the dogs alive—her body had chunks taken out of her side, and there was postmortem lividity on her face. Postmortem means blood settled in a place in the body, and it turns the skin purple. Over time, her body was rotting because it was so hot in the house.

I called the dispatcher and advised I needed a coroner. I did not notify the homicide division because it looked like the death was natural. I smelled bad from being close to the body. The dogs were given to the neighbor. The dogs had survived by drinking water from the toilet.

I went back to the station to change my shirt. When I walked in the locker room, a couple of guys were dressing, and as soon as I walked, the guys told me, "Get the hell out of here, Danna."

As soon as I changed, I was okay.

Headless Body in the Barrio

One evening, a man was walking his dog in an isolated country area of Chino. His dog found a dead body lying in the bushes, and all that was left was a skull with a bullet hole in it and a portion of the ribs. Homicide was called to the scene. They checked around for anything that would help identify the body. Nothing was found.

Homicide had a forensic expert develop the face. Using clay, she took possession of the remains and worked on it. Based on the factors found, dentures in the mouth, and the skull showing indications that the person was balding, she estimated the age of the person as being in the late sixties. Her findings severely through off the detectives who were trying to identify a sixty-year-old man, and they were never able to identify the body. The victim was eventually buried in a place known as a pauper's field where they bury unknown people.

When I got involved, I had the same information as homicide as the sixty-year-old as described above. I checked on past information of people reported missing in that area of California. I found one reported person who was in his mid-twenties. I contacted the department who issued the missing person report and asked for a photograph of the person. When I received the photograph of a young man who was balding, the next thing I did was contact the coroner for I needed the body they put in pauper's field.

I contacted the family, hoping for X-rays of the missing person. I was sent X-rays of his back area. When they exhumed the body, they X-rayed the same location on his body. When we compared the two X-rays together, they matched perfectly. Foster had bone spurs on his spine. Now I knew the identity of the dead man. He had false teeth and a receding hairline. Bingo, he was from Dennison, Ohio.

I will not mention his name so I can keep the family confidentiality for privacy. Now I had a name and contacted the family with very sad information about their relative who was a victim of a homicide. The mother was very grateful, for she now knew what happened to her son, and the family was able to properly bury him.

Now that I identified the body, I needed to catch the suspects that killed the man. Deputy Brian English had an informant who told him of a possible murder in the neighborhood. He was told the name of who did the killing, along with an unknown person. So I had connected the two who were accused of the murder. I was able to receive leave from the narcotic division to work this case. I had put a puzzle together. I had decided to move slowly as I interviewed many people. I finally lucked out and was given a name. I found out later that this person was a good friend of the suspect. I also located two women who were not involved in the killing, but they were witnesses of the murder. I found these two up in Northern California hiding from the suspect. I assured these frightened women I would put them in a secret location in San Bernardino County. I would need them to testify in court. They stated Mean Mel shot Foster, and he was on the floor near the heater. Part of the carpet was cut out revealing a blood stain. We identified samples, and it was Foster's blood. We needed the evidence to prove the truth. The car Foster's body was put in was tracked to a paint shop in Los Angeles. I looked up the shop and the guy answered. I described the car and told him not to paint it because the car was evidence. The evidence ID bureau opened the truck and pulled out the lining for blood samples. This further tightened the noose around both guys.

Eventually, I caught the murder suspect and was told he took a ring off the murdered man. They described the ring as a turquoise design, and the rest of the ring was silver or perhaps white gold. One of the suspects sold the ring to a friend who worked at a local gas station and who talked to the victim.

I asked the mother if her son had the ring, and she replied, "Yes, a turquoise ring." I asked her if I was to find it, if she would be able to identify it. She was certain she would be able to because she bought the ring for his birthday. I tracked the ring down and found the station attendant and took the ring right off his finger. He was advised the ring was stolen off a dead man's hand, and it is evidence for a murder case. He told me who he got it from, and the confidential informant gave the suspects names as Mean Mel and Jeb the Jerk.

I eventually borrowed several turquoise rings from a jewelry store to make a lineup of rings. This find made my case solid now. I had San Bernardino personnel photograph the ring and send it to Dennison Police Department to identify it. They presented the photo to the mother for me, and she was able to identify the ring. She recognized it. I found the suspects and arrested them.

I went to Dennison to find out if Foster was set up for the money. When I arrived, I was met at the airport by the police department. They were very cordial and loaned me a car to use while I was there and allowed me to carry my gun.

I asked a punk the police knew as one of the tough guys in town some questions, and he told me to go screw myself and tossed an object at me that looked like a chalkboard eraser. I stepped aside, and I went for him and gave him a hard open hand slap on his face. It stunned him. Some people call that a "gangster slap." He was shocked that I hit him.

"You can't do that to me!" he said.

I told him, "Next time, you will think twice about throwing anything at me, and I further responded that he might be an accessory to a murder."

Then I asked him, "Now, are you going to be a nice guy and cooperate—or are you going to take a ride with me to California in handcuffs?"

"Which way do you want it?" He told me.

Foster had ten thousand dollars on him and went to Chino to buy some dope for his friends, so all of us came up with the money plan. When I was there, I found a buddy of Foster's and asked him if Foster used, and he said he did not use narcotics. I used to live in the Chino area, and I could set up a transaction. I warned him he had better not make a call to California or to anyone in Chino. Then I threatened him, "If I find out you called anyone, you better not run—for I will hunt you down and have you arrested for accessory to murder." He never did make any calls. Mean Mel was working feeding livestock. I arrested him there.

The case went through the court proceedings, and the women did a great job in court and their testimony nailed both men for the murder. Both suspects were found guilty and sent to prison for many years.

This investigation was written up in a national magazine called True Police.

Headless Teen

One night I was teamed up with another deputy, and we received a call to the rural area where Riverside County and San Bernardino County meet near the dairy farms. We received a report that the body of a male was lying on the side of the road. When we arrived, we found a body without a head located, and the head was severed at the neck. We also found a wire fastened from a telephone pole to another pole directly across the street. The wire was the height where the body's head was severed.

This was no accident, the man was deliberately killed. Whether by prank gone wrong or by murder, either way, we notified another sheriff department to respond due to the rest of the investigation for the body was found on the Riverside County side. They worked on it but never solved the case. They were hoping a We-Tip would come in. They identified the body, and he was a local teenager who rode a dirt bike often and was hated by the farmers because he continually frightened the cows, causing the cows to stop producing milk. One of the farmers decided to shut down this problem for good. Probably with unintended circumstances and probably classified as a second-degree murder.

Honor Killing

Not long after the Ray murders, there was another killing, and this was called honor killing. I responded on graveyard shift to a home, and I found a female adult on the bed in the master bedroom. She sustained on wound caused by a gunshot to the head. I was later told the murder was what is called a Sharia Law, killing, it is a Moslem thing. The victim was killed by her husband because the victim's sister was having an affair with another man, shaming her husband. Her sister shamed the family, and therefore, the sister—our victim— deserved to be killed. Some of the Arabs are nuts. Now don't misunderstand me, not all Arabs are nutty.

I was tired of dealing with dead people until the homicide boys arrived and took over the crime scene. This unit had excellent men and women. Brian English was a sergeant in the division. Their motto was "When your life suddenly ends by another person, that is when their day begins."

Killing of a Six-Year-Old

It was late the day, I received a telephone call from Captain Mike Cardwell from the Apple Valley Station. I learned that he and his detectives were out on a case of a missing six-year-old. There was great concern because they had trouble believing the parents when they reported the six-year-old son missing. Their story did not make sense. When asked how long the child was missing, they replied that it had been several hours ago. The deputy who was taking the report asked why they took so long to report their son missing. They became nervous, and the deputy had a bad feeling about the parents. He felt they were lying. Suspecting foul play, the deputy reported this to his captain. The captain became alarmed and was planning a major search of the desert.

When I arrived at the command post and met with the captain—after being told the circumstances—I agreed with him. He planned to place both parents on the polygraph and felt the search was soon to be a homicide investigation. I knew who this captain was, and his crew would solve this quickly because he was one of the outstanding captains on the department. He retired as deputy chief.

He called a polygraph examiner and also requested a tracking team from the Morongo Station. I met with them for the purpose of any assistance for resources and additional manpower, etc. The captain did not need anything from me, and later, his men found the child. In addition, he had the tracker check the property for any indication that the child walked away as the parents claimed. The trackers notified the captain there was no indication that the boy ever left the property on foot. Our concern greatly increased. When the polygraph examiner arrived—one of the best in the business—the captain requested the female be first. When the examiner completed her examination, she admitted she and her husband killed their son by starvation, along with beatings.

She said the husband put out cigarettes on the boy's back for the fun of it and enjoyed making him suffer and scream from pain. The father admitted he beat the boy severely, and if he cried out, he punched him in the stomach so the marks and bruises wouldn't show. The two parents were arrested for murder. We had our mines team from the Barstow Station go down this dangerous shaft and recover the body of the poor little angel who suffered at the hands of these two monsters.

Yes, we found the poor little boy on the bottom of an abandoned mine shaft. They killed the boy and took him to this mine shaft and threw him down into it. They confessed to killing their son, and the mother blamed her husband for killing him. They were taken to jail for murder. Well, these two bastards are now in prison, and I hope they burn in hell.

I know this case is hard to believe. Yes, there are evil people out there just like these two. These two belong in the gas chamber and should be put to death. It is too bad California did away with the death penalty. I eventually got home and couldn't sleep thinking about how this little boy had no one to help him before it was too late. This kind of case is the reason I became a peace officer to catch people like these two. Yes, folks, there are people like these who can only be described as human garbage.

I included a poem at the beginning of this book because of this poor innocent child.

Macabre Wife Killing

Graveyard produced another killing. This time, it was a couple who were arguing most of the day about their finances. The husband was blaming the wife for continuous financial problems, and eventually he had reached his limits. It was time he did something to solve the problems they had and decided to solve the problem for once and for all. That night, he would kill her. They continued arguing until they went to bed. So he blamed her and planned to kill her, and by killing her, that would be a solution. He figured once you get rid of the problem, the problem is solved.

I will warn you for the following information will be hard to believe. This was what he did to the money-spending wife after they went to bed for the evening. He kissed his wife and said, "Good night, honey," when instead he should have said good riddance. He lay staring at the ceiling, thinking if he should kill her; then he made his final decision to kill her and planned how he was going to do it. He would go to the garage quietly for he did not want his wife to awaken while she was sleeping blissfully. He lay next to her, listening to her breathing—after all, they have been married for many years, and he would know by the sound of her breathing when she was sound asleep.

He then slipped from under the blankets and tiptoed out of the bedroom and went to the garage to get his favorite bat, a Mickey Mantle Slugger Baseball Bat. The bat had the words New York

Slugger written down on it, and then he held it like the great Mickey Mantle with a firm grip and brought it down with such force the blow crushed the side of her head in with blood and gray brain matter oozing out of her skull. She was still moving and shaking, and then down went the bat again—this time across her forehead. That did it, the home run he was looking for. He thought it was a grand slam. He looked around at all the blood and gray matter and thought it is going to be a big job to clean up this mess. He struck her twice more, and her left eye popped out of the socket, and then he stopped. He wished she was still alive so she could clean up her own mess.

He got a bucket and a rag and started to clean up which took at least two hours. He went into the bathroom and washed his hands. He would be doing the rest of the job in the early morning.

Mr. Nut job dragged her by her hair into the garage. He put on overalls and gloves and realized he could not carry his wife outside and put her in the car in her current condition. He went in the garage and got the saw off his workbench and then went in the kitchen to get a butcher knife. He wanted to be able to put her entire body in the freezer until he could figure out where to dispose of the body parts. The best thing to do to solve this situation was to make her smaller. Then, off went her head first, then her arms, then her legs, then it came time to cut her in two. So he continued to saw the torso in two, and then he wrapped the body parts with newspaper and placed her body parts into the large freezer and then threw her head into the freezer. Both parts of the torso he dumped into two plastic garbage bags.

This incident unraveled for him when his wife's best friend arrived at the home for a visit, and she discovered her friend was not home. She noticed the hallway closet was left open, and then she noticed her friend's clothing was missing. The closet had nothing in it that belonged to her friend. She became suspicious and looked in the garage where the body parts were stored. When she opened the freezer, she found her friend's head. She screamed then ran outside and called the sheriff and reported the find. She asked a sheriff to meet her in Grand Terrace, a small bedroom city in San Bernardino County. The suspect was out somewhere and planned on telling people his wife left him. He was captured on graveyard shift late at night.

At the time, I was the detective sergeant, so I sent Detective Floyd Gilbreth to meet with the friend. It was about one hour before I was called back by Floyd telling me, "Phil, there is something major here. I looked into the freezer in the garage. I opened an item wrapped in butcher paper that the woman told me to open up, and I found some fingers and a hand." I asked Floyd if he was sure of what he saw, and he replied, "Phil, I know what a hand looks like."

I told Floyd, "Do not go any farther into the house, secure the scene, I will be right there, and make sure the female stays with you." I will notify homicide to roll.

When I finished talking to Floyd, I went to the captain's office and told him what we had, and that I was going to the scene. I was told the first homicide detective arrived, and the entire property was taped with crime scene tape. I told Floyd to stay with the homicide detective and that we are going to turn the scene over to the homicide detectives and told Floyd to stay with him if he needs assistance. Then all the other detectives arrived. I was told the whole story of what happened. There was a husband and wife argument over money, and they both went to bed to sleep, and after about an hour, the husband killed the wife.

Before the suspect was apprehended, the crime lab investigators were called to process the crime scene the bedroom as well as the garage. When they processed the bedroom, they illuminated the room with their lighting detecting blood. The lab team found blood stains on the ceiling as well as on the furniture.

This suspect did a reenactment film for the homicide division. He went into great detail of his actions the night of the murder. It was very early, and very few people would be outside so he carried a bag out to his car for later disposal. He transported the bags to a small town not far from where he lived. This was when his plan for disposing of the body parts and was made while he drove to Las Vegas.

Dead Woman at 7-Eleven

I got a call to respond to the local 7-Eleven store. A female collapsed outside of the store, and when I arrived, she was lying on the cement in front of the store. I checked her vitals and no pulse, she was dead. I called for emergency medical to respond to the scene.

Inside the bend of her arms, she had injected something. It was clear to me she was a hype, meaning abuser of illegal narcotics.

The store clerk told us the woman was with somebody and pointed to a male adult pacing back and forth outside. I walked up to him and placed the handcuffs on him and told him he was under arrest for suspicion of murder. After I read him his rights, I asked him to roll up his sleeves and show me his arms—which had extensive tracks. Then I checked his eyes, and he was under the influence. I asked him if he used heroin, and he told me, "Yes, he did."

I asked him if he gave her some heroin, and he said, "Yes."

I believed that he overdosed her and accidentally killed her. I rolled homicide, and they soon arrived and took over at the scene. I left the scene.

Woman Found Dead

There was a murder scene I responded to on graveyard shift. An older woman was found shot to death. The victim's daughter found her propped up on the living room couch, soaked with blood and dead. I secured the scene. When I checked the woman, there were no signs of life. I notified dispatch to roll homicide, and the coroner, believing this case to be a murder. Homicide arrived, and I walked the daughter through the house after no one was found hiding, and it was safe. The deceased was well-known in the area politically. The daughter relayed the events to me.

When she arrived at her mother's home, the back door was unlocked and wide open. When she walked through the laundry room and glanced around, her eyes scanned the dark room, and she noticed a silhouette. It appeared to be a person. She got closer and reached over to turn on the lamp and was shocked. She walked to the couch and pulled back the afghan. It was soaked in blood. She grabbed the shoulder area, and the body fell forward. She stepped back and realized it was her mother. She screamed "Mom!" And then dialed 911 and then ran out in the street, yelling, "Help me!" The neighbors also called 911.

With a great deal of sensitivity, the deputy advised her she would have to wait outside because the interior was a crime scene. She understood, and while the deputy was in the process of looking on the couch and on the floor, looking for a hand gun. Just in case, it was a suicide. He did not find a gun at this point. He believed this was a murder and searched the rest of the rooms for a possible suspect still inside hiding in the room. After a thorough search, he also went outside and waited for homicide to come. While he was waiting with the daughter, he asked for her mother's name. He asked where her father was, and she replied they were getting divorced. He asked her if they were getting along, and she replied that no, they were not. The deputy stopped questioning her. He would advise the detectives what she told him about her mother and father. Later, the homicide detectives learned the victim was shot twice by two different weapons with two different caliber bullets. I escorted the daughter outside the home, and I placed her into my patrol car and explained to her the entire house is a crime scene.

After I checked the home for any possible suspects, I was asked to investigate the murder. If I would handle the case, I would have to have a homicide detective with me at all times. Who they sent was not interested in the case; he would rather be at home, and he did not work late. Other homicide detectives arrived to handle the initial investigation of the crime scene. I wanted to interview the husband who was separated from the victim. I tried to make contact with him at his residence and was told he had left to do some jogging. I wanted to wait for him to return. But the detective wanted to call it a night. I was not happy, but I had this lead.

During the investigation, the daughter pointed to the couch where the body of her mother was still lying face forward the way she left her mother when she ran outside the house. The daughter said she thought it was a revenge killing because her mother wanted a divorce, and she believed the stepfather killed her mother.

Well, eventually, I transferred and never went back to the case; and they never made an arrest for murder. It was unsolved when I retired. Sometimes you fall into investigations, and no matter how you try, you cannot solve the case, so you feel you will end up taking it with you to the grave.

Grandmother

One day, when I was six years old, my grandmother died. When she died, the funeral homes were busy, so they kept her in the living room and had the viewing in that room. The problem was I was staying with my cousins at my aunt and uncle's home, and I was sleeping in the same room where my grandmother was lying in her coffin. I was sleeping on the couch in the living room—no more than five feet from my grandmother. Needless to say, for a six-year-old, it was a scary experience especially at night. There were noises coming from her sounding like she was moving around in the coffin. One night, it got so bad that I ran into my cousin's room and jumped on his bed. After I woke him up, I told him our grandmother is a zombie. He sat on the couch and waited for what I claimed was happening. While he was out with me sitting on the couch, he heard the noise and he yelled, "Oh shit!" And then he ran back into his room, leaving me there.

My uncle came out and yelled, "What the hell are you two doing in here? Get to sleep!"

My cousin told him our grandmother is still alive, followed by me telling him his mother is a zombie. I couldn't understand why he was so angry.

He looked in the coffin and found a mouse in it. He got the mouse and carried it by its tail and threw outside, then we went back to bed. Then we heard another noise, and this time, it was a moan.

When I heard that, I ran back in to my cousin's room and told him, I heard another noise from the room, and this time, it was a moan. That is when I grabbed a pillow, and my cousin kicked me out of his bed. I slept on the floor next to his bed that night. That morning, he embellished the story, saying his reason he came back in to the room was because our grandmother was calling for him. She was calling out for Tommy to come to her later that day.

My other uncle came in to the room and grabbed me and pulled me dragged me to the coffin and lifted me and said, "See, she is dead."

Then he told me to kiss a dead body. I told him he was crazy, and no way was I kissing a dead body. I struggled out of his grip and ran outside. This uncle thought he was funny. My mother came outside to talk to me, and I complained to her. I told her I will not sleep in that room until grandmother is gone. My mother told me she talked to her brother and told him to stop scaring me. I told her that was not enough, and no way was I going to stay in that room with a dead body. My mother told me that my grandmother was leaving, and they are taking her to the funeral home. That was good news. I was not going in that house until my grandmother was at her final resting place. Everything got better over at my aunt's house, but I never forgot that incident.

The Coroner's Building

I went to speak to the coroner about the guy who was hit on the head. The suspect took his gun and hit him over the head and knocked him out behind the steering wheel.

One day, I had to be at the coroner's building and talk to him about a case I was working on. I found him cutting up a body from a plane crash. I walked up to him and began talking to him when I backed up against a stainless steel gurney and felt something touching me from behind. I reached my arm around, and when I did, an arm fell down so I had to pick it up and place it back on the gurney. I grabbed the hand of this dead guy from a plane crash and when I tried to move the arm, it would not bend or move well. Coupled with the smell, the sheet came off and the person's eyes were wide open. I had to get out of that place. It was nuts in there; dead bodies all over the place. There were a lot of bodies on gurneys from the plane crash, murders, robberies, and assaults. The morgue was packed with dead bodies, and there was no room anywhere in the morgue that night.

To the Rookie: Stay Alive

There were a few situations I got into knowing I could have been killed or sustain career-ending injuries. I consider myself very lucky that I managed to come away untouched. For example, when I was dealing with a nut like Maniac. When I was in his house, he wanted to kill me; but as luck would have it, the shotgun got wedged under the bottom drawer of his kitchen counter preventing him from getting the weapon—thus saving me from taking a shotgun blast to my face. And as I was sitting at the counter, my ankle holster and gun showed when I crossed my legs, and the pants cuff raided above the gun exposing my weapon. Maniac did not grab the ax and hit me over the head with it, and when I think of the time I was sitting on the stool talking, his hand was gripping the handle of the ax. He explained to his crime partner that he wanted to put that ax in my head but thought I could get my gun fast enough to shoot him. Well, he thought wrong, and I believed that if he grabbed the ax, he could get around the counter—rush me before I could react quickly enough to save my life. I did not know he was a suspect in a robbery in that Fontana store and the store in the city of Ontario. He could have gotten around the counter and split my head in two for the rookie learns from mistakes. I hope you remember your practical problems during your training at the academy. Always remember there are people out there who want to kill you rather than face arrest and placing yourself where you prefer working alone rather than ask for assistance is not a smart decision. You have to have help when you are arresting a dangerous person like Maniac, a cold-blooded killer and especially when you are completing graveyard shift.

Occasionally, Deputy English and I ended up on the same shift, and when that happened, we worked well together, backed each other, helped each other working on a big case. One of us would do the crime scene while the other questioned suspects. Another bad move I made was running a warrant check while standing between the suspect and a living room table. The suspect got the advantage, and he certainly used it in that incident. I should have realized that he—like anyone else—would not want to go to jail. He jumped me and began choking me, I was losing the fight. If there were no other deputies to help me, I would have been killed by being choked to death. All you "new" guys in the profession of lawman, don't get complacent and remember there are people who want you dead. Come home when your shift is over, especially from graveyard shift.

CHAPTER 5

Blackmail

We received a call one evening from the manager of a local large food store, reporting that he was being blackmailed by an unknown male subject. This person threatened the manager that if he did not place a large amount of money at a certain place to pick up, he would contaminate the food with rat poison. He told the manager to look in the cereal box, which is marked with an X, and he will see a small bundle of rat poison—just so the manager knows he means business. The blackmailer told him when he gets the money then he will tell him where the rest of the rat poison was.

The manager pleaded to us when he reported to the police not to go public with the information. If it gets out in the press, it will destroy his business. We assured him the information will not get out; however, he must tell us what his plan of action will be to safeguard the public. He agreed. He understood the public has to be warned. I told the manager to try to keep the caller on the phone as long as he can. We contacted the phone company to place a trace on any calls and gave them the store phone numbers. Then I placed a detective in an unmarked car at each public pay phone to standby to make an arrest of the blackmailer. We waited for the call to come in. We waited for about an hour after the plan was in place when the call came in. I advised the detectives the call was in progress and requested each detective to report in. All advised that they saw nothing except one who advised he spotted a Mexican male in the booth.

I told him no one is to move in yet, and only make contact with the suspect when I authorize it.

I told him, "When the caller hangs up, advise me."

The caller hung up, and I told him to move in and arrest him. He was the suspect, and the manager was very relieved that we got him. We made him identify the contaminated food, and I told him if he did not cooperate with us and point out the poisoned food, and if anyone was hurt after eating the poisoned food, he will be charged with attempted murder. If anyone was killed, he would be charged with murder. All the contaminated food was located, and the problem was resolved. The phone company verified that the call came in from that pay phone. The suspect was booked for terrorism.

Cow Dung Fire

The fire department called and advised there was a large fire and at a fertilizer plant. A pile of fertilizer was set on fire by someone, and the business owner lost the entire stock of his product. The fire was caused by gasoline thrown on the fertilizer, which consisted of dry cow dung—which is highly combustible.

I thought to myself, *It was Timothy the Oklahoman who was behind the explosion of the building that killed numerous people in Oklahoma.*

I responded to the factory in South Chino, and no one was injured during the incident, but there was a loss of the product. I met with the owner and asked him if he had names of who he believed were responsible for the fire. He believed it was his competition. I started the investigation, and the owner gave me an empty can of gasoline he found. I looked into it and found some gasoline and removed the liquid from the can and placed the gas into an evidence jar that I had for a crime kit evidence collections.

Based on thinner information from other interviews, I conducted at the plant as well as some people living near the plant. I found a person that had seen a truck belonging to the other plant down the street. That truck was seen at the victim's business a half a block away. There was a man sitting in the cab of the truck.

I asked the owner why he did not give the can to the fire department when they talked to him, and he responded they did not ask for it based on the information.

I wrote a search warrant for the sample. It was possible the competition had a gasoline pump, and I wanted to compare his gas with the small amount of gas collected from the scene. I found a judge who signed the warrant, and that day served the warrant and got my sample. I gave both samples to our lab for comparison. In about two weeks, I was notified by the lab that they had the results, and the gas matched.

Next, I moved to arrest the suspect for arson after I interviewed him, and he failed the polygraph test. I booked him for arson and advised the victim that we arrested the person who he believed it was. The fire department had the arson investigated, and everything was reconciled for the fire. I felt good I was able to solve this case and felt the fire department had been deprived of important evidence. There is no doubt the fire department would have solved it if they had the information earlier. Oh well.

Hotsy Totsy, Another Nazi

We were notified that a black family was the victim of a hate crime. For several nights, they found that someone had painted a large Nazi Swastika on their garage door. Each morning when the man of the house left for work, he found the damaged door and painted over it, only to find the same malicious damage occurring again.

When we got involved, we placed night cameras up in a place where we were sure we would get an image of the suspect. Within one day, we were successful, and we had an image of a man who lived across the street from the victim. We watched the video, and the suspect would walk from his house about three o'clock in the morning, carrying a bucket of paint. We arrested the jerk that night. He actually believed he was Adolf Hitler reincarnated. We had no trouble finding the nuts on graveyard shift.

Indecent Exposure

When I left a store, and as I was driving, I noticed a male adult in the bushes. I pulled away from the store, and he jumped out of the bushes with his pants down, exposing himself to the women near him. We call this weenie-wagging indecent exposure. I arrested him shortly, and after I took him to the station and questioned him, he began crying and told me that he could not help himself. I booked him for indecent exposure. I was busy that night. There was a full moon in the sky, and all the loons were out.

No Sheep, Just a Filly

One day, a man called the department and reported that someone raped his horse. When I was told about this bizarre case, he advised us the horse was raped during the middle of the night. We decided to position a night camera in the stall. I told the captain to tell the owner to make sure the horse is dolled up and does not look like a floozy—and maybe a little lipstick and applying fake eyelashes would be good. The captain had no sense of humor that day because he suggested that I tell the owner that myself. I knew it was time to stop joking.

We advised the detective to make sure the camera was placed in the location, and once we get a picture of this nutcase and we are able to establish a pattern, we can set up surveillance near the horse. When the suspect returns to the stable, we will nab him once he mounts the horse. We will handle this case like we do when we investigate like it is a human being. We will collect the semen from the horse's vagina. The owner asked us why we told him that we were going to nail a crazy man and send him someplace where he can get help. We are going to get a veterinarian to help us following the incident and hoped to capture the suspect's picture.

We set up surveillance on a Sunday night and waited until our rapist of horses arrived at the stable, carrying a small stepladder. He climbed the stepladder, and once he reached the top, he dropped his pants to his ankles then he lifted the horse's tail up and entered the animal. The horse looked back once and slightly kicked back. When he had enough, Casanova and the horse, we grabbed him. He tried to run but he ran into one of the detectives. We brought the horse to the vet. With us, he swabbed the area necessary.

The oversexed suspect was taken to Ward B, which was a mental health holding facility, and we placed a hold on him. We wanted to book him with the proper charge and send him through our court system. As the case was proceeding through the system, the suspect was sentenced to a mental health facility, and we figured he would pay dearly when he had to explain to his wife. And after the civil hearing, he would have to pay damages to the horse owner. He was ordered to pay the county for the cost of the investigation and the veterinarian bill.

Native Demonstrations at River

I received a report there was rioting at the river. The Needles Station was responsible for patrolling the river. The sheriff advised us there were demonstrations at the Colorado River by a local tribe of Chemehuevi Indians. They were protesting the nuclear storage site. Their concern was the water could become contaminated by nuclear waste because the water level was near the surface.

The concern I had is that they were going to block the freeway and go into the City of Needles and cause civil unrest. The Indians said they were going to close part of the Colorado River and charge the public for that part of the river because that part of the river was their territory. It is called Copper Canyon and is where most people gather for the Easter Holiday.

The sheriff and I attended a meeting with the tribe, and we sat there and listened to their threats; and when finished, we stood up and blasted the group and said, "If you try to stop people from going to the river, somebody is going to jail."

We told them it is a public area, and you can't charge people to go to the river. Just before we entered the building, I told the sheriff not to call them Indians but to refer to them as natives, American Natives. We were going to tell them we will be watching for any violations. The very first words he said were "You Indians."

Protestors

One day, I was contacted by my captain who was in charge of the Needles Station. He notified me there was a group of people who were protesting against the proposal to put radiation waste in the ground near population centers. Although this waste is going to be placed in deep tunnels, encased in cement to eliminate the radiation seeping into the ground and contaminating the water table under the ground, they were worried that the contamination would poison many people.

The company held a town hall meeting to reassure the public there was nothing to worry about. They were told the company was an expert in the procedure of disposal of radioactive waste.

That information did not sway the group. The company put on dog and pony show with slides of the process, but it did not convince the group who attended the meeting. They decided to disrupt the meeting and were eventually thrown out. This small group went to the proposed site a few days later and began to demonstrate. If they failed to stop the operation, they planned to throw themselves in the hole where the radiation was to be dumped.

I met with the leader, who was not playing with a full deck, and explained to him that if any one trespassed or interfered with the operation while the company was handling dangerous radiation, they would be placed under arrest. He advised me they would demonstrate in downtown Needles. I told this man if he and his group tried anything stupid, I was going to arrest him. I first made contact with him at his campsite late on graveyard shift on an unannounced visit. I surprised them for they were not expecting me. I found they were trashing the area they set up as their camp. I gave them until daybreak to clean up their mess, or I would impound their cars and arrest them for illegally dumping trash.

We thought they would block the freeway (I-40) and continue to cause civil disorder all the way to the City of Needles. I advised them if they tried anything in the City of Needles, they would be arrested. I asked if they thought causing problems would work with the highway patrol officers arresting violators. The CHP would never allow them to disrupt the freeway from normal operations. I warned them not to turn the desert into a garbage dump. I told them to pick up the trash, or I would come back that evening and take some people to jail with the leaders of the group.

I kept my promise and arrived by sheriff helicopter on graveyard shift. Soon after my arrival, federal rangers who were responsible for this section of the desert, ordered the people to clean up the mess, and one of their leaders stepped up to me and told me they wouldn't comply. They soon learned I don't mess with the Feds, and furthermore, they shouldn't mess with me. I spun this spokesperson man around and slapped the handcuffs on him after the Feds requested me to take him into custody for littering Federal Land. He was placed under arrest for assorted federal codes, including interfering with the law, a violation of PC 148. He was taken to Needles jail, and once he arrived, I gave a citation release in Needles thirty miles from the campsite. Problem solved. I was making it very expensive for him to get back to the campsite. This time, morning hours worked for my benefit for both charges and citation violations.

I returned the following morning and found the entire group had left the area and cleaned up their mess. They never caused trouble with the company or the City of Needles again. Most of these people were nice people who were misinformed. The government never used the proposed site. Local politics prevailed.

The radiation was from the county's hospitals and happened when their X-ray machines produced some waste radiation byproduct.

Girls Gone Wild

Frankly, this part of the river was a problem for us because of nudity. Normal people were trying to enjoy boating with their families and friends. The captain of the Needles station was receiving complaints that there were sex acts occurring in public, and the girls would strip completely and dance on the decks and boats. One day on boat patrol, I asked the deputies if they enjoyed the duty working boating violations, and I asked one of them why they liked that patrol, and they said because they wanted to keep the river area cleaned up and for the area to remain safe for the public. I replied, "It was not those nasty naked women?"

The Indians never carried out their threats, and eventually, we cleaned up the problem. The girls moved to a sandbar located away from Copper Canyon.

Wild West

Fontana is a cop's dream for it is loaded with bad guys. Several years ago, it was like the Wild West because of the Kaiser Steel Plant. There were bar fights galore with those steel workers, and there were a lot of tough guys. There was every kind of crime. Robbery, kidnapping, attempted murder, child molest, and there were notorious motorcycle gangs like the *Hell's Angels*, *Vagos*, and *Righteous Ones*—and they all lived in Fontana

The area still had a lot of crooks when I arrived at that sub-station. I teamed up with Johnnie Powell, and it was not unusual for both of us to make a good felony arrest. Johnnie was working a caseload that was burying him, and when I got there, I took some of his caseload. John appreciated my help, and the captain gave us freedom to do whatever it takes to catch the crooks. I remember walking into the squad room, and deputies were filling out paperwork with the suspects they had arrested for being involved in a big fight. One bozo was sitting in front of one of the deputies, and this man had a perfect bite out of his ear. Someone managed to take a bite out of him during a fight.

The action never stopped at that station, that is why the sheriff placed Captain O'Rourke there. Mike was given the tough assignments, and he was given those assignments because he was able as the watch commander to get the crew on a mission to clean up the streets of dirt bags. He was able to accomplish this and get the station to get better results. He and the sergeants and deputies formed a successful team, and the detective division increased their level of arrests. Many of the arrests were for in-progress crimes.

The sheriff let Mike solve the problems. Before he was assigned to the Fontana Station, he was sent to Victorville, a real ball-buster because they were short of men and the response time was too long for the public satisfaction. He had his hands full, and the crime rate was out of sight for the crew at the station. Before he made captain, I had the opportunity and was lucky to work for him, and all he wanted was for us to work hard and do the best we could. He was simply a great sergeant. I have always admired this man, and when I made sergeant, I wanted to be as successful and lead as close as possible, providing this style of leadership at the west end area of the county.

Fontana has come a long way, and there are plenty of good places to live in that city now. With the sheriffs' office and Fontana Police working together, they have done a great job of cleaning up the entire place.

CHAPTER 6

Missing Nine-Year-Old

It was a mild summer night up in Big Bear, a winter resort town in the large mountain range in San Bernardino County where a young nine-year-old boy was missing. He was last seen in a small park not too far from the sheriff's substation.

The boy disappeared, and hours later, the parents reported him missing. So we began one of the biggest searches in the history of the department. I had every search team in my region, as well as three mounted horse teams spread out through the area. We made flyers to hand out within the community. In the darkened hours, the search continued on. We did a computer check for every child molester in the area of the park and had a record of a serial child molester who liked little boys. We zeroed in on him, but we could not come up with anything. To this day, the boy is presumed dead.

Missing Ten-Year-Old

It was a hot summer night when we were notified a ten-year-old was missing. He took off with an ATV out into the desert. It was just getting dark, and we wondered why the father allowed him to leave. The camp citizen volunteers arrived for a search team. It was pitch dark, and there was a full moon. It was very dangerous at night. I told them to follow the dirt road, and they should find the tire tracks then follow the tracks. We found the boy in good shape. He ran out of gas. I explained in the desert there are abandoned mine shafts that go straight down. Sometimes they go down around one hundred feet. If your son were to drive over the opening, we would have brought back your son dead. He was found within six feet from where the ATV stopped just in time near a mine shaft.

Missing Family

Death Valley is a forbidding place—a beautiful place—but if you are not careful, it will swallow you up. You could disappear forever.

Case in point: A family of five has not been seen since their fatal day trip to Death Valley. They were from Germany; two adults and three children. They drove into Death Valley and disappeared. Their relatives called from Europe reporting to the police the family members went to this forbidding place and were lost or missing.

Inyo county sheriff department called San Bernardino county sheriff for they needed help searching for the missing family. San Bernardino mounted search teams. They organized another massive search for the family but were not successful and found no trace of the family. So I deployed the Barstow Station search team to assist them. Then a pilot flying over the valley spotted the family's car abandoned in a very remote canyon. They couldn't possibly have survived. We went to the car and found several shoe prints going away from the car. The trackers followed the prints until they vanished completely. We spent four hours trying to pick up the tracks but no luck. There was nothing around the car that left any clues. We searched the entire weekend, and nothing was found. No tracks, nothing, it was as if they disappeared into thin air.

Why did they drive to such a remote place? Our trackers could find nothing, and these men are considered the best in the country. It was getting late, and we had to leave the area before it got pitch black.

The family car was towed to the Inyo Station for clues, blood, notes, cameras, and any evidence. We were asking ourselves why they parents went to such a remote location? It was miles from other people, so why did the parents endanger the family especially the children? Where did the father take his family? We speculated maybe they found an abandoned mine, and once they all got into the mine, it caved in on them trapping them all. We checked all the maps for mine locations and claims. The only thing I am sure of is that they are all probably dead from exposure.

The family in Germany wanted their family members back, and it was very sad that we could not find them after two large searches.

Missing Persons

I was contacted by the Barstow Station that they were searching for a missing adult man from the City of Barstow. The personnel found the subject's car abandoned, and a camera near the car. The film was developed, and the photographs revealed the subject with an unknown female and an unknown male subject. I was batting zero on these searches. It was now graveyard shift's responsibility throughout the county.

Another Missing Person

I was notified by Rancho Cucamonga about another missing person with a mental disability. The station requested assistance, but I had to turn them down because all my search teams were out on searches. About an hour after that, I was notified by the station that they found the person. That was a great relief to me.

The General's Relative

I had a telephone call from the Needles Station, advising me they were going to start a search in their area. I could not believe my ears. Not another search. It took the station several hours to find the missing subject who was the son of a general was going to send military personnel and send military helicopters. We advised the general that we have our own helicopters. The station deputies found the missing man dead. He was lying among some bushes, and we told the general there was no need to send anyone to assist us in the search. The captain of the station broke the sad news to the general that night. That night for me was crazy. The next day, I was able to catch up on paperwork.

Tarantula

Brian English and I worked together. We exchanged information about the people who were committing crimes in the beat. The beat that we worked mostly was designated Area 1, and that covered most of the county area of Chino. We worked with same informants, and we kept our promises to people, so they felt they could trust us to never give up the identity of our informants. I felt that a patrol officer cannot be successful without the information that enabled us to solve crimes in the area.

Sometimes, there are some funny things that bring humor to the job. One day, a friend named Don flagged me down to talk to me about his teenage daughter. He asked if I could keep an eye out and help him keep her out of trouble. I told him I would do my best to help him, and since Brian usually worked the beat, I asked him to assist Don also.

I remember one evening, we stopped to talk to one our friends in our beat at the beginning of our graveyard shift. We stopped at our friend's house, and Brian met with Don Jurrard. He was asking for assistance with his typical teenage daughter. It was not often she got in trouble in the local neighborhood. She was never involved in anything serious, but she was out beyond curfew, and he was worried because he smelled alcohol on her at times. Every time it was late, and if we saw Bev, we would place her in the patrol car and bring her home to Don. We did something with a team approach, and it worked because Bev grew up to be an outstanding young woman.

One day, Bev called Brian and said she wanted to talk to him, and he rolled up to her in the unit. It was a hot swing-shift day, and he had his window down. When he rolled up to her, she placed a large ugly, hairy tarantula on his lap. Brian started jumping around the front seat. I looked at Brian and asked if he was having a seizure?

He kept yelling, "Get it off me!"

And I replied, "Are you kidding, I am not going near that thing, it will bite."

"Just slide out of the car," I told him.

He followed my instructions and got out with the spider still hanging on his pants. I told Brian it was still on him and that is when he began this strange dance I can only describe as a "jumping up and smacking" his lap dance. Our friend asked Brian if he wanted me to shoot the spider off him.

The spider finally fell off of him, and the next thing he did was started running and yelling, "Where is she?"

I told our friend that his daughter was getting out of control and ought to get her in the house and hide and lay low. I said "Don, I know Brian real good, and he is going to look for that brat."

Bev ran up to Don and me, looking for protection from Brian. I told her she was on her own, and she better hide inside the house. She ran. Brian walked up to me and Don, and the first thing he asked was "Where is she?"

I asked, "Who?"

Brian asked, "Where is Beverly? She threw a big tarantula spider on me."

She ran in the house, and Don told her, "Not in my room."

Don asked Brian if he was afraid of a little spider. "Yes," Brian replied "This thing has eight hairy legs and was about six inches long and had two big black eyes that stuck out of his head, and it is still in my patrol car."

"Well, I guess you are now on foot patrol."

And I told him "I am not going to give you my unit. I hate spiders and ants."

We both asked Brian if he could teach us the dance he was doing in the car while the spider was on his lap.

He said, "Very funny, now let's go it's almost the end of our shift."

Then Don told Brian he could not go into his house without a search warrant. We had fun, but he was not laughing. Brian told me, "You need to see it."

I said, "No, thank you, I am afraid of spiders and ants. They both bite."

Bev came out of the house and apologized. Brian told her, "The next time you do that, you are going to get arrested for trying to kill a police officer. Those spiders are poisonous."

I responded, "Only if you eat one."

Beverly has grown up to be a good citizen and a great mom with her children. Don and his wife did such a great job raising their daughter. Brian and I were lucky to have known that family. I never did find out the name of that dance Brian did. I think he would have rather been in a gunfight then deal with that big ugly thing.

Flying Rocks

I was in the office during graveyard shift, and I received notification from a dispatcher who advised me a deputy wanted to meet at his current location. I left the station to meet with the victims. I arrived at a home in Grand Terrace, a small community north of San Bernardino. I found my deputy, wearing his riot helmet, and followed him into the backyard. I found the entire family wearing helmets. There was a male adult wearing a football helmet, and his wife was also wearing a football helmet. Their two sons were wearing bicycle helmets. The family car windshield was protected by a sheet of plywood as were the house windows. When the deputy told me what was going on, he said mysterious rocks have been flying into their property, and the rocks are coming from an empty field. As the deputy was talking, another rock flew and hit the house wall made of stucco and took a large chunk out of the wall. The wife said the rocks flew into the home and traveled around comers together, and the rock hit her on the head, and she said, "These rocks can think."

Rocks flew into our bedroom while we were sleeping. I asked her, "Did the rock knock first?"

That stupid remark angered her, so I apologized.

All I was thinking is the rocks possibly came from a farther distance. It appeared to be coming from an adjacent field. I had deputies widen the area, plus the helicopters widened the search. All attempts failed to succeed in finding a suspect. I called off the search because other calls were backing up.

I called these victims weeks later to check on them. A priest went to the house and blessed the home and visited the family on a regular basis. I suggested the best people to contact would be the city maintenance crew because the empty field belonged to the city. I explained to the family I would continue to find out a cause for the flying rocks. The deputies and I left unable to give a solution to this crazy case. I thought to myself, *Between the nude lady sitting on top of a refrigerator while killing a live rabbit as she spoke an unknown language, and the flying rocks coming from nowhere, I will be glad when I retire.*

The case was never solved.

Crazy Woman on Top of a Refrigerator

It was the latter part of graveyard shift when I received a strange call, and I was instructed to meet a man in his backyard. When I arrived at the home, I walked through a chain link gate and proceeded to the backyard. As I stepped around the comer of the house, that is when I made contact with a man who ran up to me. I stepped back quickly and told the man, "Hey, take it easy."

The very stressed man complied. He told me that his wife is possessed by the devil, and he wanted help. I asked him, "Where is she?"

He replied, "She is on top of the refrigerator."

I said, "Well, let's go in, and I'll see what I can do."

I asked, "Does she live in the home?" I advised at that point, "If she legally lives in the home, I cannot force her out of her home."

I walked into the kitchen and found her sitting on top of the refrigerator naked. The kitchen has a high ceiling, so there was enough room to allow her to sit on top of the appliance. I told the husband to give his wife some clothing to wear. The woman was holding a dead rabbit. I asked her to come down from where she was, and that was when the woman ripped the rabbit's head off and threw it at me. I had rabbit blood on my clean uniform. I told the husband, "This crazy woman is yelling in another language."

I called the paramedics and figured they could get to her down without hurting her. I completed a 5150 form, which meant I could request a temporary hold on her while she is being examined by professionals. The husband asked if I knew of any priest that does exorcisms. I told him no, but he can get some holy water from his church and ask for a gallon and ask for the priest because she is going to need plenty of water. She was taken to ward B of the mental health facility for a temporary seventy-hour hold and for an evaluation.

The Bug Rules

I just started my shift and was driving to my assigned beat when a call came in that was not on my beat. When I responded, the address was located in a well-groomed residential neighborhood. I made contact with a woman who was at the front door, and she invited me inside. I walked into the kitchen and sat at the kitchen table. The call was to report a stolen bicycle.

As I was writing the description, a bug landed on my pad. It was a roach. I looked up to the ceiling, and there were many roaches crawling on the ceiling. I looked on the kitchen counter and it was full of roaches running around. On the stove as well as, there were several of them walking on my shirt. It was at that point that I decided to go outside to finish talking with the lady. When walking out, I noticed children's toys on the floor next to the front door, and I asked her if I could see the children. She asked why, and I told her I wanted to see if the children were in the home. She became very frightened and nervous. I calmed her down and told her I just wanted to take a quick look. She took me to the first door from the kitchen, and when she opened the door, I saw a baby crib across the room. I walked up to the crib and shined the flashlight on the baby. There were several roaches walking on the blanket as well as on the baby's face. I was instantly alarmed because the roaches were walking next to the baby's mouth, which was open.

The mother said, "My God, please don't take my baby away, poor baby."

I asked her to calm down and told her I was not going to take her baby away for now but told her I would not be doing my job if I did not safeguard your baby from the entire bug problem inside her house. I asked if she had family nearby, and she told me yes. I suggested she call them to come over to her house and help her clean it up and told her to get rid of the bugs.

"Call an exterminator," I told her. I assured her I would be returning later, and if I found the house in the same condition, then I would have to request the child protective services agency take the children for safekeeping.

I told her that I know roaches enter the house with paper bags and come in from the outside. You must keep your home very clean with no dirty dishes on the sink or dirty diapers piled on the floor. All you are doing is making it pleasant for them to be in the home. I explained what a roach egg looks like. They are very small and square and white. When they hatch, there could be more than one hundred roaches in your house. I asked her if she wanted the roaches to lay eggs and did she want to have the eggs in her baby's mouth.

I returned as promised, and the house was spotless. Her mother walked up to me and told me she was going to file a complaint. I told her my name followed by giving a suggestion for her daughter. Her daughter walked up to her mother and told her "Don't you dare threaten the deputy, he did a great favor for me."

Lemonade

The detective invited John to his home, and when both walked in, he told John to have a seat in the living room. His wife was in the kitchen, and he told her, "Honey I am home."

And he requested a glass of cold lemonade for his buddy. She replied, "No, and don't bother me!"

He replied, "Honey, I am not kidding, really, bring the lemonade here."

She said, "No and don't bother me."

He repeated the request to his wife, and she told him he must be hard of hearing. John told him to forget it, and he said, "She is not going to get away with it."

John told him, "Maybe we should get back to work and forget about the lemonade." John told him he didn't want to be in a position of being in the middle of their argument. This detective was not going to lose this battle with his wife again for cold lemonade, then John said he was going to the car. Then he walked outside. He yelled at his wife, "I mean it—you better get that glass of lemonade."

She yelled back "No! Don't bother me!"

Johnnie described what went on in the house. It sounded like WWII at that house. Then John heard a glass crash on the wall, and suddenly, the detective came charging out the door, yelling, "I am sorry, why are you mad at me? I didn't do anything."

175

And there was another sound of glass crashing against the door. Then he told Johnnie, "I think I am in trouble". Johnnie suggested he lie low and bring her a box of candy.

He said, "I am going to give her something all right, a broom so she can fly around with a pointed black hat."

When Johnnie told me the story, it was so funny. Johnnie went back to the station, and I could not stop laughing. John suggested if I get offered a glass of cold lemonade to say, "No thanks. You are in the wrong business."

Synopsis

This book describes several calls that patrol officers experience while working graveyard shifts. There are several bizarre problems and dangerous incidents. The graveyard shift is unique to many family fights because of the use of alcohol. Often, these fights are violent. The book describes the danger for the officer when he must solve the problems before he leaves to handle another call. The reader will understand when darkness arrives, the danger increases. It is a lonely shift as the deputy slowly drives his patrol unit while looking for criminal activity in his area. Now the cat and mouse game begins as he is fighting fatigue and trying to stay alert for the next call.

The book describes the danger he is put in. Suddenly as he patrols, he is confronted with a man planning a suicide. On another call, a violent man jumps the deputy and tries to kill him. The officer is suddenly fighting for his life as the suspect attempts to get the officer's gun.

The book describes crimes against people and very violent incidents when the officer arrives at the location and makes contact. The people who called for help end up being the victim, trying to solve the dispute between two or more persons within a few minutes—and at times, the situation makes it worst. Usually, someone either needs medical attention or someone goes to jail. The officer must solve the problem before he or she makes the arrest. That is when the violence begins and when injury is caused upon the officer. If the people would cooperate, I guess that is why as human beings we have divorces and wars, and we have jails and law enforcement officers.

When people stop talking that is when the trouble begins. When marriage is failing, there are gambling problems, or the biggest problem of them all—arguments over money issues, teenagers when they are out of control, loss of job—just to list a few. We used to tell the husband to take a walk, get them separated while they cool down, had the wife go visit a friend, or go to a relative and take the kids with them. When the law changed, a family dispute had to be solved before the officer left, and if there were any physical altercations, someone goes to jail and a full report is made.

The book traces a typical graveyard officer with his assigned calls and up the end of his/her shift when the officer returns to the station. Before he goes home, he dedicates from his notes once he has completed the paperwork, he will in-basket and mark the case number. The next day, clerical personnel will take the recording and place the case number in the log listing all reports. The reports will eventually be reviewed by the watch commander, and he will mark the on the list of the report numbers, indicating the report has been reviewed. The report will then be typed and reviewed, completing the report and then sent to the complaint officer and his job is to read reports and then take them to the district attorney. He will discuss the case with the district attorney to get a criminal complaint against the suspect. If by any chance the reviewing attorney rejects the report on the grounds that the case needs further follow-up, a copy of the rejection slip will be given to the officer to complete. Once the report is accepted, it will be forwarded to the court and the jail. Soon a preliminary hearing will be held for the defendant as he begins to go through the criminal system. Then on graveyard, the officer begins his hunt for another criminal, and the cycle begins again. The officer hopes everything will go smooth, so he does not lose any sleep.

Most officers are rigid, for they must follow the guidelines in the Penal Code of their state. Felony convictions take much more time to investigate. Lesser crime violations are quicker to handle, then infractions. All crimes reported take time to investigate. During graveyard, the notes of the crime must be taken quickly because there are fewer officers on duty, and it just works that way. There are many officers that park in a high crime area, and some nights it is very slow and quiet, and many will park their unit and do reports.

The mere presence of the police car will usually stop the criminal, or they will get caught. As a rule of thumb, when a person is driving through a business section or residential area slowly or sitting there at two o'clock in the morning, they are begging to be stopped and checked out by the officer. The officer works with probable cause before he or she makes his contact. This person as an example traveling by car or walking through a high crime area at 2:00 a.m. is suspicious behavior. The officers usually check the identification and run a warrant check, then smells the suspect's breath, checks his eyes, and checks his pockets for weapons. They don't search the car unless there is good reason like he sees something inside that is a violation of an order, or he smells something that he believes the driver to be driving under the influence of alcohol or narcotics. During graveyard shift, there are many drunk-driving arrests and crimes against persons in bar fights.

During graveyard, the criminals begin moving around the community, looking for something to take without paying for it. The cover of night gives a disadvantage over the patrol officer. A good officer knows evil is lurking around, looking to commit the perfect crime. Crooks will slowly pass the store front windows, planning to get in and remove the owner's property—if not for personal selling then stolen to sell to a fence. A fence is a person who accepts the stolen property for quarters on the dollar and sold at a nice profit either out of his garage or at the swap meets or at the local truck stop. I am not saying the third working truck driver is not a crook. I am saying the local crook will spend time at a truck exchange with stolen items and with another local thief.

The pimp will be nearby supervising hookers, and he is more than willing to buy stolen goods, and it is usual to find the vice squad working the truck stops. It's a vicious circle. Many of the prostitutes know the fence, so vice puts the squeeze on them, and she eventually rolls over—which means cooperates with law enforcement to keep out of jail. To be honest, very little stolen property is recovered for the victim. Sometimes law enforcement just gets lucky, and we are able to find and recover the stolen property, but it is a difficult thing finding who owned the property. That is why law enforcement gives safety fairs to teach how citizens should mark their property with their license number, name, and phone number. And photographing the property helps. All of this will help to get your property back promptly. Otherwise, it is sold at a police auction. Bicycles are given away during Christmas to children who come from poor families.

Once I was cruising in a commercial area, which was a high crime area, and I checked out a walker in a dark area with buildings and noticed he was coming out between two buildings, so I made contact with the person and asked him what he was doing walking next to a closed building. He began shaking nervously, and I flashed a light from my flashlight on his eyes, his pupils were very constricted. I determined he was a hype. This is a narcotic user on heroin, meth, speed, or some substance; and they inject the substance in their veins. It was no doubt he was looking for something to steal, so he is able to get his dope.

In the business of law enforcement, the officers deal with "close calls" due to the nature of the job and where the action is. The only problem is where the action is an injury could happen that would cause the officer to retire early in his career as a police officer/deputy sheriff. Danger occurs from some type of law enforcement action, firemen responding, and medical emergency workers going toward the emergency. When the citizens run away from emergency floods or, terror attacks, such as 9/11 in New York City, these disasters cause the loss of many emergency responders. The officer in this book had several close calls, and it was pure luck that nothing happened. When the suspect in another similar situation, and when the officer makes an error in judgment, a bad shooting, or a car accident killing, the driver and the occupants anything can turn to a close call. For instance, the book describes one event that occurred in front of an officer, and he could not fire his handgun when deadly force was needed to save a life of a child. Quick thinking stopped the deadly assault from continuing. A car pursuit at a very high rate of speed with red lights and sirens could cause a necessary action to occur, and there is a tremendous liability including serious injuries. Lawsuits begin costing the city or county several thousands of dollars and up to a million dollars. When the defendant officer is found at fault, there could be punitive damages against the officer causing the loss of his home and his freedom.

This book will describe where the graveyard patrolmen are needed, there is a chance of extreme danger for the officer when making contact with people during the early morning darkness. From the beginning of the eight-hour graveyard shift, the graveyard officer could be involved in several car stops. This is because the bars are closing, and the person who has been consuming alcohol is very easy to catch while under the influence. The rule of thumb is if the driver swerves over the lane lines and is spotted, the officer pulls behind the vehicle and follows the car a short distance. Looking for more probable causes to make the stop and may have another reason to stop the car if the driver is alternating speeds and the taillights are frequently on and off as the driver steps on and off his brakes. It is time to make a vehicle stop. As the officer advises the dispatcher of the stop the graveyard officer waits until the driver is near a well-lit area and then activates his red lights and the driver eventually stops. The officer positions a spotlight on the side where the driver is located, and the officer steps out of his patrol car slowly and approaches the driver. He illuminates the back seat of the vehicle as he approaches the driver. He begins to tell the driver why he was pulled over and stopped and requests the suspect's driver license. He smells the driver's breath for alcohol or marijuana and asks him to step out of the vehicle and to perform a short test. If under the influence, he checks the eyes and looks for bloodshot eyes. If the pupils are constricted, it could mean under the influence of an illegal drug. The driver is requested to show the inside of both his arms. The officer looks for needle marks. These are called "tracks." The person is determined to be under the influence of an illegal narcotics, and there are signs including obvious injection marks made over a vein and sometimes done over tattoos for the purpose of concealing the injection. Sometimes they will inject themselves between the toes.

At the end of the shift, the traffic violations begin, speeding and reckless driving, and minor fender benders happen. The calls begin to come in reporting commercial burglaries.

The officers are assigned to handle these calls, and you will read about real incidents that include murder, rape, and robbery.

The assignments reveal the extreme dangers in the early morning while you and your family are asleep safely in your bed. Graveyard shift officers have many different experiences. The patrol officers are solving many crimes and dealing with societies problems. This book has a collection where several calls for service were unfortunate where the deputy sheriff was too late. Villains use the cover of darkness to prey on innocent people, and the graveyard patrol officer will hunt and smash evil between the 911 calls.

All the cases mentioned in this book are factual and will give you a snapshot of the actual events a person goes through in the academy to become a police officer as well as on patrol. The instructors teach the cadet it is better to use the voice instead of the fist. Although I have had my share of physical confrontations, I never looked for one.

Disclaimer

This book is not intended to be totally factual and is based on recall of true cases and may be a multiple case combination. This is a personal journey of one cop as he describes everyday encounters with people pursuing criminals and aiding victims. Some names and places have been changed to protect the innocent and to avoid giving notoriety and to maintain anonymity.

I have tried to recreate events and recall actual conversations but not in great detail. The author and publisher has made every effort to relate the memories of actual and similar cases, and we do not assume and disclaim any liability to any party for loss, damage, or disruption by errors or omissions whether from negligence or any other cause.

The End

About the Author

Phillip Danna was born in Brooklyn, New York. His parents moved to Long Island from Brooklyn when he was a child. He grew up in Long Island during his preteen years and then moved to California.

After he graduated from high school, he attended Cal Poly University majoring in mechanical engineering. He left Cal Poly and attended Columbia College in Los Angeles and studied television directing.

The war broke out and he joined the Navy. He attended UDT Seal School in Coronado Island and was almost through when he injured his knee two weeks before graduation. That injury was caused by falling on some large rocks during what is called a rock potage. This meant pulling a raft out in the ocean and as I was doing this a big wave came and knocked him backwards. Part of the training was to do runs on the beach with a raft over head and because his knee was injured, he had a hard time running on the beach sand. That problem caused him to be dropped out. He was transferred to the admiral's barge. It was a ceremonial duty to take the admiral around to the ships in the bay so he could attend various meetings. He was the bow hook on that boat. Eventually, he was honorably discharged from the navy.

They told him that he could come back and finish the training once his knee was repaired. However, he decided to get out of the Navy and start his civilian life. He found a job in a few days after receiving my honorable discharge and joined a retail company. Later, he became a district manager for the company and had to transfer thirteen times although each time it was for a promotion. While the company promoted him each time, he was tired of being moved so he decided to find a job that would keep him in one place. One night after he finished merchandising inventories and drove home very late, he spotted a deputy changing his flat tire. He noticed that the deputy needed help and pulled behind him, putting on his headlights. He talked to the deputy for a while and asked him how he liked being a police officer. The officer replied that he loved it and recommend that Phillip looked into it. The very next day he was able to fill out an application. In seven months, he was hired as a Deputy One and went through the Sheriffs' Academy class. He turned his suit in for a uniform. The physical testing was easy after being in UDT. He graduated in the top five of his class.

Phillip retired after twenty-five years on the force with a rank of Deputy Chief of patrol of the High Desert and mountains. When he retired, he joined FEMA and traveled to Guam, Saipan, and Rota, a small dot in Pacific Ocean and Chuuk Island. During WWII it was named Truk Island and Tinian was the island where Enola Gay took off when it carried the atomic bomb and bombed Hiroshima.

Phillip wrote this book because he wanted the public to what a police officer does when the day darkens and graveyard begins.

We were all kidding around before hell week. Once hell week began there was no goofing off anymore."

10-8

CPSIA information can be obtained at www.ICGtesting.com
Printed in the USA
BVOW08s0818090316

439652BV00003B/147/P